Contents

Part 1 Living in a digital world

The Open University

TU100
My digital life

Block 6
My world

This publication forms part of the Open University module TU100 *My digital life*. Details of this and other Open University modules can be obtained from the Student Registration and Enquiry Service, The Open University, PO Box 197, Milton Keynes MK7 6BJ, United Kingdom (tel. +44 (0)845 300 60 90; email general-enquiries@open.ac.uk).

Alternatively, you may visit the Open University website at www.open.ac.uk where you can learn more about the wide range of modules and packs offered at all levels by The Open University.

To purchase a selection of Open University materials visit www.ouw.co.uk, or contact Open University Worldwide, Walton Hall, Milton Keynes MK7 6AA, United Kingdom for a brochure (tel. +44 (0)1908 858793; fax +44 (0)1908 858787; email ouw-customer-services@open.ac.uk).

The Open University
Walton Hall, Milton Keynes
MK7 6AA

First published 2011. [Second edition 2015.]

Edited and designed by The Open University.

Typeset by SR Nova Pvt. Ltd, Bangalore, India.

Printed in the United Kingdom by Latimer Trend and Company Ltd, Plymouth.

ISBN 978 1 7800 7994 3

2.1

Part 1
Living in a digital world

Author: Mike Richards (with Mustafa Ali, John Woodthorpe and Chris Dobbyn)

Introduction

So far in TU100, information technology has been presented as the solution to a large number of problems: finding information, generating and delivering medical and scientific information, creating and serving entertainment, enabling communications, creating whole new communities and so on. These are solutions to problems felt by the same Western industrial societies that invented modern information technology – making up less than a third of the world's population.

It is not necessarily the case that these technologies appeal to, or are needed by, the majority of people who live in different societies. Human society is made much richer by the incredible diversity of cultures. We live in a world of countless languages, religions, economic and social orders, opportunities and threats. Can new technologies that have done so much to improve our own lives also be of benefit to hunter–gatherer societies whose lifestyle has seen little change in tens of thousands of years, as well as the hundreds of millions of people rushing to the new megacities of Asia and Latin America?

The fact that different levels of access to information technologies exist around the world is known, broadly, as 'the digital divide'. This term is used so widely in news reports and magazine articles that authors often neglect to say what it actually means. Yet as you will discover in this part, the concept of a digital divide is a surprisingly complex one.

In this part you will learn more about what is – and, perhaps, what *should* be – meant by 'the digital divide'. In fact you'll learn that rather than thinking about a single digital divide, it is much better to think of many divides that can be found not only between rich countries and poor nations but also between individual citizens and even members of the same family.

Throughout this part, you will be applying many of the skills and ideas that you have learned throughout TU100. Many of the concepts you have met previously will reappear in this part, providing you with a chance to consolidate your understanding of them.

> Note: Session 5 of this part, 'Nepal – a case study in connection', is an online study component involving videos and a third-party web resource. You should allow about 2–3 hours for this online study, which can be accessed from the resources page associated with this part on the TU100 website.
>
> The rest of the part also includes several videos and other online activities. You may choose to complete these at the end of each session or as they occur in the text.

Learning outcomes

Your study of this part will help you to do the following.

Knowledge and understanding

- Describe the concept of a digital divide and some of its different aspects.
- Describe the different scales of the digital divide (local, national and global).
- Describe approaches to technological development in a number of different countries and explain the reasons for these approaches.
- Describe the roles of government, private industry, communities and individuals in bridging the digital divide.
- Explain the importance of the digital divide in relation to other divides (e.g. cultural, political, economic, etc.).
- Describe some of the social, political and economic factors influencing the digital divide.

Cognitive skills

- Analyse examples of appropriate technology in the context of the digital divide.

Key skills

- Use appropriate statistical techniques to analyse aspects of various digital divides.

Practical and professional skills

- Locate, evaluate and use information on the Web.

The digital divide and the wealth of nations

1

In the introduction I indicated that many complexities lie behind the term 'digital divide'. To begin this part, then, you will explore some of the ideas associated with the term. Then you will consider some factors – in particular, wealth – that may be connected with a digital divide.

1.1 What is the digital divide?

As you have seen in previous blocks, for many technical subjects the Wikipedia entry is a good starting point for further research. So to provide a way in to the discussion in this session, I used Wikipedia to find a definition of the *digital divide*. When I accessed the relevant page, the first two sentences read as follows:

> The digital divide refers to the gap between people with effective access to digital and information technology and those with very limited or no access at all. It includes the imbalance both in physical access to technology and the resources and skills needed to effectively participate as a digital citizen.
>
> Wikipedia, 2011

Yet, as you might expect, there are complications to this simple picture. For a start, the Wikipedia definition may be considered to be too wide, because it is unclear which 'digital and information' technologies are being referred to. On the other hand, 'information technology' indicates that, despite its name, the term 'digital divide' may encompass certain non-digital technologies. So there is a sense in which the term 'digital divide' itself can be considered to be too narrow.

In this part I will take the view that the basis of the digital divide is exclusion from modern ICTs: lack of access to mobile phones, or even to conventional analogue telephone networks, can be as formidable a handicap as lack of access to powerful computers and the internet.

Two digital divides

The world rarely conforms to simplistic definitions. The idea of a *single* digital divide may be neither useful nor accurate, as the following activity will show.

Activity 1 (exploratory)

Refer back to the Wikipedia definition given above. What are the two main inequalities that it encompasses?

Comment

The definition refers to the following:

1   inequality in access to the necessary hardware, software and connections – the physical resources required for digital access

2   inequality in the necessary skills required to use digital technology.

So, to focus my discussion here, I will concentrate on the following two aspects of the *digital divide*:

1   the gulf between people who have *access* to, and the *resources* to use, ICTs and those who do not

2   the gulf between people who have the *skills*, *knowledge* and *abilities* to use ICTs and those who do not.

Analysing the digital divide

The digital divide is of interest to academics from many disciplines – to engineers and computer scientists, but also to sociologists, political scientists, economists, cultural theorists and others. They all have their own perspectives on the topic, and naturally this has generated an enormous amount of literature, with countless different understandings of the issue. We may have to accept that there are many different divides, all with the same outcome – unequal access to new technologies.

For example, the ICT analyst Eszter Hargittai (2003) goes even further than my definition, identifying two further digital divides:

•   between those who control the production and distribution of ICTs and their content, and those who do not

•   between those who own ICTs and their content, and those who do not.

Another commentator, the academic Bharat Mehra, defines the digital divide as 'the troubling gap between those who use computers and the Internet and those who do not' (Mehra et al., 2004, p. 782). His definition is somewhat similar to Wikipedia's, but it has a judgemental element to it – that the existence of the divide is a cause for concern. This leads to a key question, and one to which I will turn next: why – if it exists at all – should the digital divide matter? One possible reason is the relationship between a nation's digital communications resources and its *wealth*.

1.2   The wealth of nations

Even if you have never travelled abroad, you might fairly confidently predict that it is harder to access telephone networks, computers and the internet in some countries than in others. But is such a prediction correct?

We need some statistics, and fortunately there are plenty. The most authoritative are those compiled by the United Nations (UN) as part of its

Millennium Development Goals. The UN monitors the world's progress towards solving its fundamental problems by regularly recording a set of *indicators* (measures) for every nation. These include infant mortality rates, vaccination rates, rates of access to education and measures of citizens' relative freedom from persecution. And amongst these indicators are measures of access to communications technologies such as fixed-line telephones, mobile phones and the internet.

Figure 1 shows, for every country and territory in the world, the percentage of citizens who have access to the internet. It is ordered along the horizontal axis from those countries with the highest rate of access to those with the lowest. The chart is colour-coded to group countries into broad geographical regions.

You had some practice at interpreting column charts like these in Block 2 Part 5.

Take a look at the figure and then try the following activity.

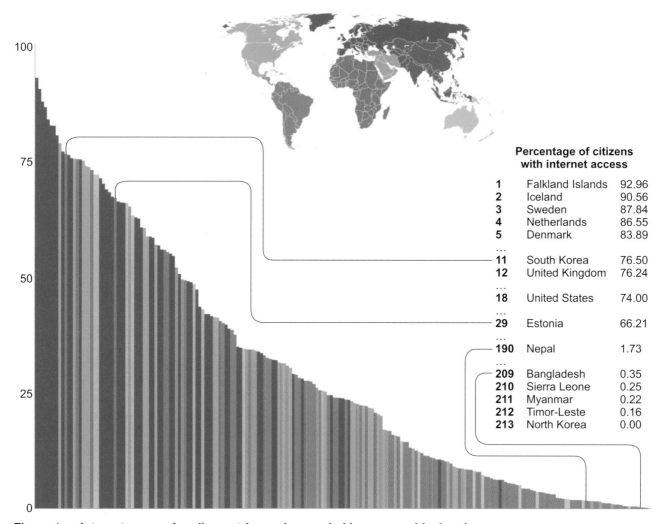

Percentage of citizens
with internet access

1	Falkland Islands	92.96
2	Iceland	90.56
3	Sweden	87.84
4	Netherlands	86.55
5	Denmark	83.89
...		
11	South Korea	76.50
12	United Kingdom	76.24
...		
18	United States	74.00
...		
29	Estonia	66.21
...		
190	Nepal	1.73
...		
209	Bangladesh	0.35
210	Sierra Leone	0.25
211	Myanmar	0.22
212	Timor-Leste	0.16
213	North Korea	0.00

Figure 1   Internet access for all countries, colour-coded by geographical region

Activity 2 (self-assessment)

What do you think is the main point that the chart makes? (Don't think about the significance of the colours at this stage.)

Among other things, Figure 1 shows that a Falkland Islander is nearly six hundred times more likely to have access to the internet than a citizen of Timor-Leste – and even more likely than that to have access than a citizen of North Korea (see Box 1).

Box 1 North Korea and the internet

In 2011, North Korea was the least connected country in the world. Its totalitarian government forbids citizens to access the internet. The country's Kwangmyong network constitutes a country-wide intranet, but it has no interconnection to the internet and most North Koreans are forbidden to use it, even if they have a computer capable of doing so. Satellite internet access is available within North Korea, although again almost no citizens can use it, and there is a single internet café in the capital Pyongyang.

The government of North Korea does have an external web presence, publishing news, tourist information, business opportunities and propaganda through a number of websites – most of which are actually hosted on servers in Western Europe and Japan. The North Korean government even has its own Facebook and Twitter accounts, although again, neither service is available inside the country.

Activity 3 (self-assessment)

Now look at the distribution of colours in the chart in Figure 1. What conclusion might you draw?

In my answer to the previous activity I said that European countries are predominantly wealthy whereas African countries are generally poor, but on what basis can such a statement be made? Before we can start to analyse how the concept of a digital divide might be related to wealth, it is important to know what 'wealth' really means.

Measuring wealth

Economists have developed a number of ways to measure the 'wealth' of countries. Most familiar is the *gross domestic product (GDP)* – the total value of the goods and services produced by a country in one year. Ranking countries by GDP, the five richest in 2010 were as shown in Table 1.

Although GDP is the simplest measure, there are profound disagreements over the precise values and hence the ranking of countries.

Table 1   Five richest countries in 2010, ranked by GDP

Rank	Country	GDP (million US dollars)
1	United States of America	14 624 184
2	People's Republic of China	5 745 133
3	Japan	5 390 897
4	Federal Republic of Germany	3 305 898
5	India	2 965 000

2010 figures compiled by the International Monetary Fund (2011)

The UK ranks seventh on the list, with an estimated GDP in 2010 of US$2 259 000 million. Yet although the UK's GDP is smaller than India's, individual citizens of the UK are generally much wealthier than those of India. So GDP is in part a reflection of population – the population of India is far greater than that of the UK – which makes it a misleading indicator of actual wealth.

Note that all monetary values in this part are given in US dollars rather than the different local currencies, to allow for ease of comparison.

A better measure of wealth, then, is *GDP per capita* (or *GDP per head*), in which a country's GDP is divided by its number of citizens. If we now list the five richest countries according to GDP per capita then the table looks very different, as shown in Table 2.

Table 2   Five richest countries in 2010, ranked by GDP per capita

Rank	Country	GDP per capita (US dollars)
1	Qatar	88 232
2	Luxembourg	80 304
3	Singapore	57 238
4	Norway	52 238
5	Brunei	47 200

2010 figures compiled by the International Monetary Fund (2011)

The UK ranks 21st with a per-capita income of US$36 298 (as a demonstration of how misleading the earlier GDP figure was, India ranks 137th with a per-capita income of just US$1176). However, even this measure does not give the true story, since it takes no account of how a nation's wealth is distributed – is it widely spread or concentrated in the hands of a few super-wealthy individuals? – or what contribution it makes to the wellbeing of its citizens.

Bodies such as the UN use a more complex method of comparing the prosperity, or development, of countries with dissimilar economic and social backgrounds. This is known as the *Human Development Index (HDI)*, and it ranks countries on a number of indicators – including measurements of life expectancy, literacy levels, educational attainment and standard of living – rather than on income alone. The range of possible HDI values is between 0 and 1, with the most developed countries having the highest values. In 2010, the provisional HDI value for the UK was 0.849, placing it in the 'very high' development category. Based on HDI, in 2010 the five most developed countries in the world were as shown in Table 3.

The final 2010 HDI figures for all countries may not be known for several years. Until all the statistics needed to calculate HDI are available, provisional figures are the best we have.

Table 3   Five most developed countries in 2010, ranked by HDI

Rank	Country	HDI
1	Norway	0.938
2	Australia	0.937
3	New Zealand	0.907
4	United States of America	0.902
5	Ireland	0.895

Provisional 2010 figures compiled by the United Nations Development Programme (n.d.)

Again using HDI, in 2010 the five least developed countries in the world were as shown in Table 4.

Table 4   Five least developed countries in 2010, ranked by HDI

Rank	Country	HDI
165	Mozambique	0.284
166	Burundi	0.282
167	Niger	0.261
168	Democratic Republic of Congo	0.239
169	Zimbabwe	0.140

Provisional 2010 figures compiled by the United Nations Development Programme (n.d.)

Wealth and internet access

With HDI established as a reasonable measure of a country's prosperity, we can try to find out to what extent access to ICTs and the skills to use them are related to wealth. Let's focus on internet access.

Activity 4 (exploratory)

I have extracted two sets of statistics from the United Nations Millennium Development Goals and collected them in the spreadsheet file internet_income.xls. (The set of internet access statistics was used to plot Figure 1 above.)

The spreadsheet file and the instructions for this activity are provided in the resources page associated with this part on the TU100 website. Open the file and examine it. Then follow the instructions to plot another kind of statistical chart, known as a *scatter chart*, based on these figures.

When you've plotted the chart, write a couple of sentences in your learning journal outlining what you think it suggests about the relationship between internet access and national wealth.

Comment

My version of the chart is given in Figure 2.

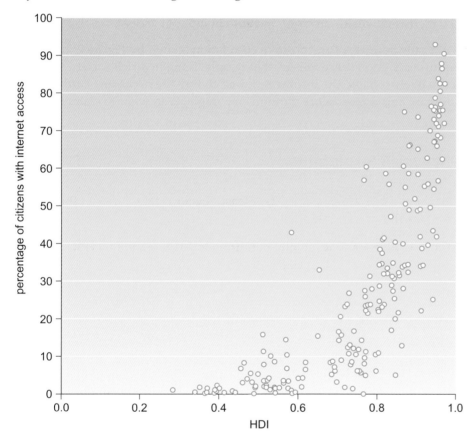

Figure 2   Scatter chart of internet access against HDI

Although it is not perfectly clear, the distribution of the points suggests that there is a correlation between the degree of a nation's access to the internet and its national wealth.

You saw in the previous activity that a scatter chart is a visual representation of how well two sets of values are correlated. In this example, the two sets of values are HDI and percentage of citizens with internet access, each country being represented by a distinct point on the scatter chart. If the two sets of values are not correlated at all, the points should be randomly scattered across the graph; if there is a correlation, the points will clump together to imply a relationship or a trend. In Figure 2 the points are clearly not randomly scattered, but rather seem to suggest a line that curves steeply upward, indicating a positive correlation: the richer a nation (in general), the greater (in general) its access to the internet.

You learned about correlation in Block 2 Part 5.

So we can certainly agree that there seems to be a general correlation between wealth and access to the internet. However, we might be tempted to go further and claim that

(1) increased wealth *causes* an increase in internet access

– not only because of the positive correlation shown by Figure 2, but also because common sense tells us that people living in a rich society are more likely to have the income required to buy the necessary hardware, software and access. More daringly, we might even want to claim that

(2) increased internet access *causes* an increase in wealth.

Activity 5 (exploratory)

Can you think of a common-sense basis for the claim that increased internet access causes an increase in wealth?

Comment

There are many possibilities. I considered the fact that internet access makes communications easier, and ease of communication facilitates the development of businesses – more customers can be reached, for example. In addition, demand for the internet results in an increased demand for well-paid IT jobs.

If claim (1) is true then we have a mildly interesting sociological observation. However, if claim (2) is true then this has much more serious implications. It means that rich societies are rich *because* of their digital resources, and that while a digital divide persists the gulf between rich and poor will endure, and probably widen. Certainly, the assumption of many commentators is that claim (2) is true, and therefore that the digital divide is a matter of great political consequence and it is vital that the divide is bridged.

Of course, these claims are not necessarily mutually exclusive: a certain amount of wealth may lead to increased internet access, which may lead to increased wealth, leading in turn to increased internet access – and so on.

Activity 6 (self-assessment)

Should we be cautious about making causal claims such as those in
(1) and (2)?

Digital divide – between and within nations

Gross inequalities of ICT access and skills between nations are generally
known as the *global digital divide*. However, a 2002 World Economic
Forum report found that 88% of all internet users lived in the more
developed countries of the north (representing only 15% of the world's
population), and so some commentators have described the global digital
divide as a 'north–south' divide.

The concept of a global north–south divide between highly developed and
less developed countries originated in the 1980s. As originally drawn, the
'north' comprised the USA, Europe, Japan and Australasia, with the
'south' constituting the remaining countries. The picture has become
increasingly complex in recent years, with a number of countries in the
former 'south' experiencing their own rapid development.

Yet this picture is complicated again by the fact that a country's economic
ranking does not mean that *everyone* within that country will find
accessing information equally easy (or difficult). Even in countries with
the very lowest levels of digital communication, it is still *possible* to use
mobile phones or the internet. Indeed, there is no part of the world where
it is physically impossible to access information, although it might be
unaffordable to all but a wealthy minority, or withheld from all but a
select few as in the case of North Korea (see Box 1 earlier).

So here is another face of the digital divide –inequalities of access and
skills *within* nations. Putting these factors together, we can begin to
represent the situation in the form of a grid.

	Inequalities of access	**Inequalities of skill**
Between nations		
Within nations		

Although the causes of such inequalities are many and complex, it is
possible to use common sense and general knowledge to suggest what
some of them might be. Thinking of inequalities of access between
nations, for example, you might come up with the following possible
factors.

	Inequalities of access	Inequalities of skill
Between nations	Low GDP Political instability and war Poor governance and corruption Disease, e.g. AIDS	
Within nations		

Activity 7 (exploratory)

In the remaining three boxes in the grid above, note down some of the possible causes of these inequalities.

Comment

I made the following suggestions.

	Inequalities of access	Inequalities of skill
Between nations	Low GDP Political instability and war Poor governance and corruption Disease, e.g. AIDS	Inadequate educational systems Nature of the national economy, e.g. largely agricultural
Within nations	Individual poverty Gross inequalities of income Unbalanced economy Civil war	Unequal access to education Low social mobility Cultural factors

You may well have thought of other valid causes. Although it is relatively easy to place causes inside individual boxes, in real life the dividing lines are not always clear-cut. For example, cultural factors might have an impact between nations as well as within them.

It is clear that many of the possible causes I listed in the previous activity are fundamentally related to national wealth. Stable and well-governed societies are more likely to be wealthy; wealthy societies, on the whole, invest in universal, high-quality education, training and technologies.

Thus far you have seen that the causes of the digital divide are myriad, complex and likely to be interrelated, with many of them related to inequalities of wealth. Now that you have seen some causes of digital divides, it is almost time to see how they are being bridged. But before we start, it is important to raise a few awkward questions.

1.3   Some questions

At a superficial level it seems unarguable that digital divides must be closed. Giving people access to ICTs would appear to bring them improved communications and increased prosperity, and transform their ability to function in an increasingly global society. But, as always, it might pay to be cautious: before insisting that everyone joins the digital society, we should pose four provocative questions. Would closing the digital divide:

- be possible?
- be desirable?
- cure poverty?
- really matter?

I'll return to these questions in the final session.

1.4   Conclusion

In this session you considered the concept of a digital divide and discovered that rather than being a single phenomenon, there are many digital divides on a number of differing scales ranging from between countries to between citizens of the same country.

The most commonly researched divide is that between countries and it is widely believed that this is related to their relative wealth. You used statistical techniques to identify a positive correlation between the relative state of development of various countries and their citizens' access to the internet.

I concluded by raising a number of questions about the importance of the digital divide. To give you some insights of your own, which might be useful in arriving at your own answers to the questions raised above, in the next session I'll look at the experiences of four parts of the world that have attempted to close the divide.

This session should have helped you with the following learning outcomes.

- Describe the concept of a digital divide and some of its different aspects.
- Describe the different scales of the digital divide (local, national and global).
- Use appropriate statistical techniques to analyse aspects of various digital divides.

2 The digital divide: connecting four nations

In this session, I will present a set of case studies that describe four different national experiences of closing the digital divide by connecting people – to the global information pool, and to one another. You will see that these case studies involve four different starting points, and four different attitudes and paths to connection.

I want to start, though, by considering a concept relevant to these case studies: that of *appropriate technology*.

2.1   Appropriate technology

The term *appropriate technology* refers to technological solutions that take account of the actual cultural, political and economic circumstances of people, aiming to improve their wellbeing whilst putting as little strain as possible on their environment or finances, and causing minimal disruption to their everyday lives. There has been an increasing emphasis of late on appropriate technology in the context of poor or developing societies, because many previous well-meaning projects to transplant technologies from developed societies to less developed regions have not been very successful (see Box 2 for an example).

Box 2 Sending PCs to the developing world

Obsolete PCs from Europe and the USA are regularly sent to developing nations where they can be put to work in schools. Many of these machines fail within months and need skilled and expensive repairs. The cause of the failure is extremely simple – the machines were designed to be used in temperate climates at low temperatures, at relatively low levels of humidity and in largely dust-free, often air-conditioned offices. When they are moved to warmer, damper climates without air-conditioning, the heat, moisture, dust and microorganisms begin to attack the computer's components, eventually resulting in complete failure. The fragility of conventional PCs in such conditions was one of the driving forces behind the design of the OLPC XO-1, which you met in Block 2 Part 2.

It is often mistakenly believed that appropriate technology means *low technology* (i.e. the opposite of *hi-tech*). Whilst many early appropriate technologies were relatively simple items such as improved wood-fuelled stoves, wind-powered water pumps and basic electric generators, there is now a turn towards appropriate *high technology*. For example, the Canadian charity Light Up the World Foundation provides LED light bulbs to developing countries. LED bulbs are manufactured in the Western world using advanced techniques, but are still an appropriate technology in much of the developing world since they offer greatly improved lighting at much lower cost and with much greater levels of safety than conventional kerosene lamps.

Activity 8 (exploratory)

You have probably heard of wind-up radios; you may even have one in your own home. The first wind-up radio was the Freeplay, invented by Trevor Baylis and introduced into rural South Africa in the 1990s. What is the key aspect of this product that made it an appropriate technology in this context?

Comment

The key aspect is that the radio did not rely on either batteries or mains power, both of which were hard to come by in rural South Africa. Instead it could be powered by the user 'winding it up' (turning a crank by hand).

2.2   Connecting Africa

The media portrayal of Africa is often one of despair and misery; yet whilst parts of the continent remain mired in real hardship, many countries are experiencing an economic boom. An end to a number of long-standing wars, a gradual turn towards democracy and a demand for Africa's natural resources have resulted in growth for many nations, raising people out of extreme poverty. For the first time, millions of people have the money, the opportunity and the desire to use ICTs.

However, Africa remains the least connected of all the inhabited continents. African nations generally have very low levels of access to fixed and mobile telephone connections, and to the internet. So the first challenge is actually to connect Africa's people to one another and to the rest of the world.

Cables and satellites

Before 1962, intercontinental communications were limited and expensive. Immense lengths of copper cable had been laid on the ocean floors, but these carried relatively little data very slowly, and with a very poor-quality signal. Using them was correspondingly expensive: in the mid-1960s, a three-minute London to New York call had to be booked in advance and cost £3, at a time when the average weekly wage was just £25.

In 1962, the satellite Telstar 1 was launched. It lasted only a few months before being crippled by radiation from a US high-altitude nuclear test, and in fact satellite communications only became practical some years later with the development of geosynchronous satellites (which remain stationary over a fixed point on the Earth's surface). Nevertheless, from this time onward satellites increasingly carried television signals across oceans, allowing sports events to be televised live and news media to broadcast up-to-the-minute information. They also carried telephone traffic: the price of international calls plummeted, even as demand soared.

Satellites continue to have an important communications role, being widely used for television and radio signals. There is also a small market for satellite telephony and satellite internet communications – for workers at sea and the military, and to serve remote areas. It is estimated that between 2009 and 2018, the worldwide market for constructing and operating communications satellites will generate nearly US$180 billion.

Despite all this, however, modern satellites carry less than 1% of the data passing between continents. They have largely been made obsolete by submarine fibre-optic cables, which carry vastly more data at much lower cost. Today, every continent except Antarctica is linked to the others by a web of cables (Figure 3), most of them laid in the last twenty years, chiefly under the Atlantic and Pacific oceans. The North Atlantic cables are the oldest and busiest, since they link the world's wealthiest regions.

West Africa, East Africa and Southern Africa are regions of the continent that each consist of several countries. In contrast, the Republic of South Africa is one of the countries in Southern Africa.

Africa is now entirely circumscribed by fibre-optic cables. In the Atlantic, huge amounts of capacity have been added by two new cables linking West Africa's fast-growing economies with Europe. In 2009, the 9500 km GLO-1 cable was completed. It is capable of carrying voice and data traffic between equatorial West Africa and the UK at a rate of 640 Gbps. The following year a 7000 km cable called Main One linked West Africa to Portugal, adding three times as much capacity again. As some indication of the growth in capacity, in 2011 the WACS cable between the UK and South Africa was completed; when fully activated, this will offer nearly nine times the capacity of the three years older GLO-1. Figure 4 shows the vast difference between Africa's submarine cables in 2009 and the planned state of affairs in 2012.

One of the most ambitious new cable projects is Seacom, a US$650 million 17 000 km link between Southern and East Africa and the Middle East and India. Before Seacom was laid, bandwidth in East Africa was extremely limited; many businesses could only access high-speed internet services through satellite. In 2009, a typical 1 Mbps satellite link (slower than domestic broadband in the UK) in Tanzania typically cost US$3000 per month, making internet access unaffordable for all but a wealthy elite and

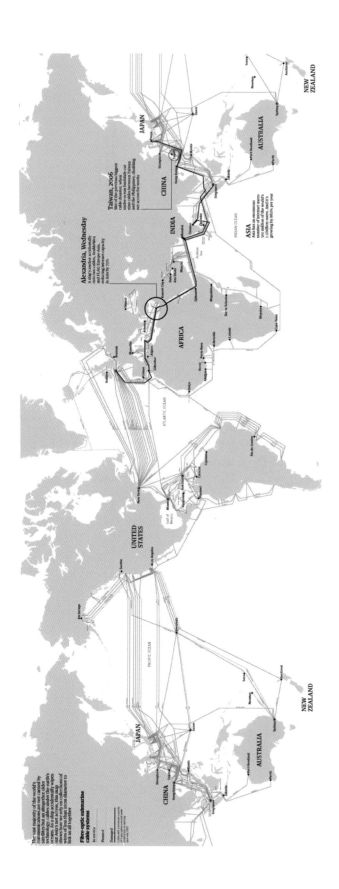

Figure 3 A map of the world's major submarine cables

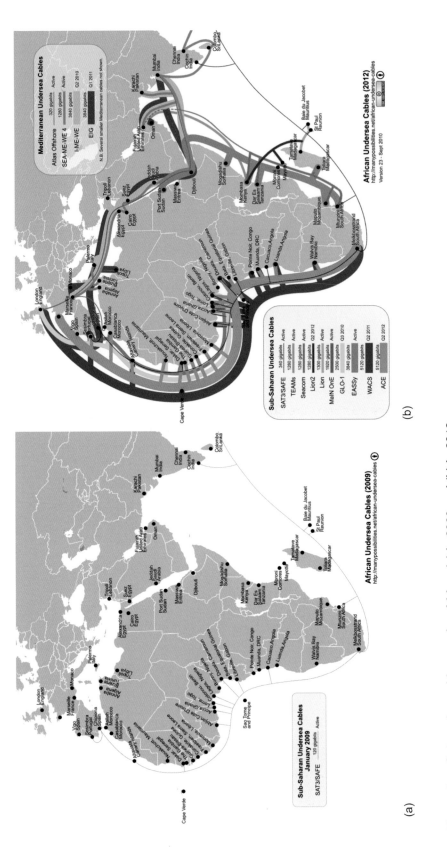

Figure 4   Submarine cables serving Africa: (a) in 2009 and (b) in 2012

a handful of businesses (in 2009, Tanzania's GDP per capita was just US$496).

Activity 9 (exploratory)

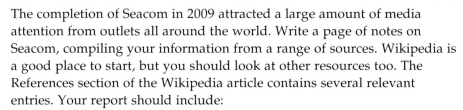

The completion of Seacom in 2009 attracted a large amount of media attention from outlets all around the world. Write a page of notes on Seacom, compiling your information from a range of sources. Wikipedia is a good place to start, but you should look at other resources too. The References section of the Wikipedia article contains several relevant entries. Your report should include:

1   technical information about the cable, its owners and where it reaches land

2   some information about how the cable will be used

3   some quotations from potential users of the cable and those who were involved in the project

4   your sources

5   links to further reading.

Comment

1   The cable has a maximum capacity of 1.26 Tbps.

   The cable's operators are SEACOM, a consortium made up of 76.25% African investment (mostly telecom operators) and 23.75% investment from Herakles Telecom, an investment group specialising in African projects although headquartered in New York.

   The main landing points for the cable are Marseilles, France; Sidi Kerir and Ras Sidr, Egypt; Djibouti, Djibouti; Mombasa, Kenya; Dar Es Salaam, Tanzania; Toliary, Madagascar; Maputo, Mozambique; Mtunzini, South Africa and Mumbai, India. The cable's operators also have agreements with other cable operators to send traffic to the UK, Namibia, Botswana, Lesotho, Swaziland, Zimbabwe, Uganda and Rwanda.

2   The cable will be used to deliver telephone, high-definition television and internet data. An especial aim has been to offer cheap 'bulk' broadband access to ISPs, allowing them to reduce the cost of internet access for end users.

You should have been able to complete items 3, 4 and 5 on your own.

Laying a submarine cable is an extraordinarily expensive undertaking, requiring thousands of kilometres of perfect optical fibre and laser signal amplifiers, all of which must work for decades under several kilometres of ocean. Some cables are commissioned and owned by a single company (GLO-1 belongs to the Nigerian telecommunications company Globacom);

many others are joint projects between the manufacturers of telecommunications equipment, telecoms companies, banks and national governments. For example, the US$700 million ACE cable linking France with most of West and Southern Africa was constructed by a partnership of fifteen private and national telecoms companies and three national governments.

An obvious shortcoming of submarine cables is that they can serve only the periphery of any continent. In developed regions, submarine cables are linked to national fibre-optic networks. But in Africa, even where fibre-optic networks exist they are restricted to particular regions; there is no continent-wide network of high-capacity cables. Botswana and South Africa have the most developed fibre-optic networks, but these serve only urban areas. Most of rural Africa has no access to any wired telephone system. In these places, wireless networking is providing links to the outside world.

South Africa: wireless community networks

South Africa Size: 1221 037 km^2 Population: 49 991 000

GDP per capita (rank)
30 000

US$10 243 (77)

HDI (rank) 0 — 1 **0.683** (129)

Internet access (rank) **8.43%** (149)

Mobile phone subscriptions per 100 people (rank) **90.60** (91)

All figures 2009

South Africa has some of the most well-developed telecoms in Africa. It has extensive fibre-optic and satellite communications, but these services are far from universally available. The country is rugged, with many sparsely populated areas, and the effects of apartheid's deliberate neglect of the black population persist. Most cities are surrounded by poorly planned townships, home to migrant labourers from the South African countryside and millions more (often illegal) workers from neighbouring countries. The country's infrastructure languishes far behind the needs of its population.

Wireless *mesh networks* (see Box 3) are being used to provide connectivity across entire communities. Some of these *community networks* are purely intranets, whilst others have links to the internet. South Africa's growing number of community networks are promoted by the Wireless Access Providers' Association, an umbrella group that shares expertise amongst community-based groups who wish to create their own meshes.

Box 3 Mesh networks

In a conventional network, such as in an office, school or home, a number of computers share the network, with messages being directed to their destinations by a dedicated router. This allows for very high-speed traffic, but suffers from two drawbacks: firstly, dedicated routers are expensive; and secondly, if the router fails then the entire network becomes useless.

The mesh network is a potentially cheaper solution whose mesh topology makes it much more resistant to failure and interruption. A mesh is an example of an *ad hoc network* in which every computer acts as a router. Data moves towards its final destination by hopping from machine to machine. Meshes are slower than conventional local networks because of these hops, but they are extremely reliable: when one computer leaves the network or crashes, others will continue to direct traffic, so a mesh network is said to be *self-healing*. In addition, as soon as a new machine joins the mesh it will automatically start to provide routing services for its peers, meaning that the network should become faster.

Mesh networks can be entirely self-contained, or they may have a connection through one or more *gateway* machines to an outside network. The mesh allows scarce resources to be shared between users: rather than each machine having a printer or an internet connection, for example, these resources are available to all the machines in the mesh. The machine hosting an internet connection or a printer gives up a small amount of its processing power and memory to run those tasks.

Mesh networks have been used extensively in military applications, but more significantly in the developing world. In the latter they are being used to build community networks in areas that lack conventional infrastructure, or where access to wired connections is either expensive or scarce. Mesh networking has become especially well established in South Africa.

You met the concept of a mesh topology in Block 3 Part 1.

An animation showing the operation of a mesh network is available in this part's resources page on the TU100 website.

The Mpumalanga mesh

Just one example of a community network is the Mpumalanga mesh (Figure 5), serving Peebles Valley on the outskirts of the Kruger National Park in the far north west of South Africa. The area is remote, extremely poor and suffers from meagre infrastructure. The mesh itself is a collaboration between South Africa's Council for Scientific and Industrial Research and the United States Agency for International Development. The mesh is centred on the valley's AIDS Care Training and Support (ACTS) clinic, which is home to an existing satellite internet connection. It was established by adding a wireless *node* to the clinic's own network, and then further nodes at a local school and a hospice. Each of those nodes is connected to a router that directs traffic on an internal network. Since the creation of the original network in 2005, the mesh has been expanded twice more, bringing further parts of the valley within reach.

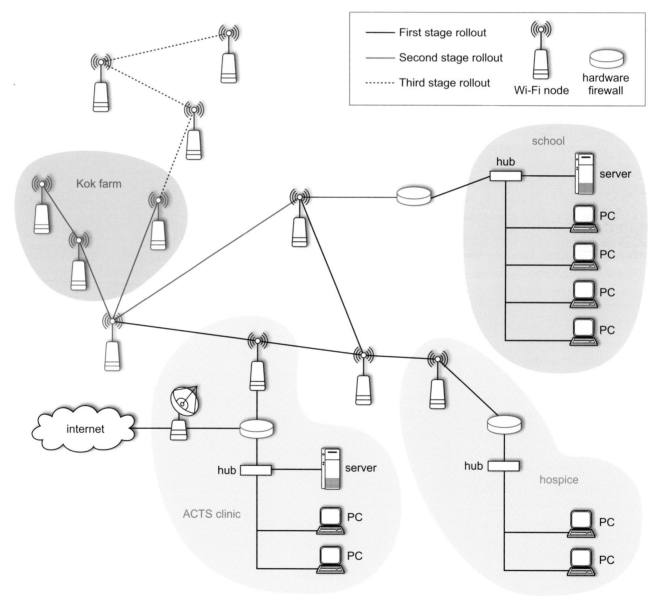

Figure 5   **The Mpumalanga mesh**

Incredible ingenuity has created meshes across inhospitable terrain. A particular problem has been the limited range of the low-power wireless signals themselves. Obviously, more powerful transmitters would give greater range, but these are expensive. An alternative is to use a *waveguide*, a device that directs wireless signals in a precise direction, greatly increasing their range. Commercial waveguides are expensive, so instead the Mpumalanga mesh (in common with other South African networks) uses what has – inevitably – been called a *cantenna*, a discarded metal food can containing a normal Wi-Fi antenna (Figure 6).

Figure 6   A cantenna wireless node being installed in the Mpumalanga mesh

Activity 10 (self-assessment)

List the characteristics of the Mpumalanga mesh that make it an appropriate technology.

Village Telco

The Village Telco community telephone system demonstrates that South African meshes can become commercially successful. Village Telco grew out of a project in the Orange Farm, a township of some 300 000 people south of Johannesburg with few basic utilities. The network allows anyone to make a free telephone call within the community, so there is no discouragement to call a doctor or school. Calls outside the community can be placed using a pre-payment system that charges less than conventional operators.

The Orange Farm system is an example of *mesh telephony*, in which a mesh network – rather than a wired or cellular network – is used to carry telephone calls. The network is built from specially designed routers, which can convert analogue speech into digital data and direct network traffic. Each router has a standard telephone connector socket that can accept a normal handset and costs about £50.

Following the success of Orange Farm, the charitable Shuttleworth Foundation and the Dabba telecom company founded the Village Phone scheme. Under this scheme, for an investment of about £300, someone – perhaps a shop or internet café owner – can install a router, called a *supernode*, that is connected to either the telephone network or the internet. They can then set up a pay phone service in the hope of recouping their investment in around six months. Any number of customers may then buy their own individual routers in exchange for a one-off fee. As soon as a customer's router is plugged in, they are allocated their personal number and connected either to the supernode or to another router in the mesh. Every person who joins the network extends the Village Telco system's reach and reliability.

Activity 11 (self-assessment)

Why do more nodes in the Village Telco system mean greater reliability?

Village Telco is currently the cheapest way of creating a telephone network anywhere in the world. It does not rely on large telecoms operators and can provide telephone services within a community even if there is no link to a nationwide telephone system. Under the name Mesh Potato (Figure 7), Village Telco is being deployed in a number of South African communities as well as in Timor-Leste. As an illustration of the flexibility of mesh networks, the Australian company Serval has adapted Village Telco into a mesh telephone system that can be quickly deployed in disaster areas where conventional telecoms networks either are absent, are inadequate or have been destroyed.

Figure 7   A Mesh Potato mesh telephony router

2.3   South Korea: digital heaven?

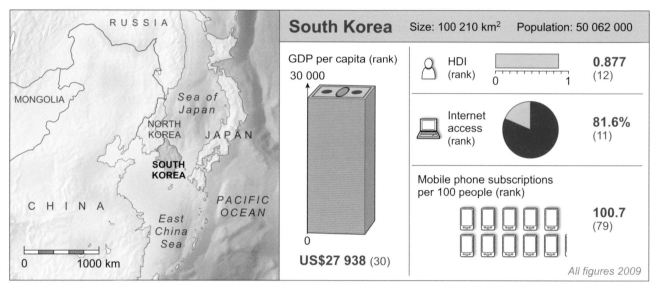

South Korea	Size: 100 210 km²	Population: 50 062 000

GDP per capita (rank)
30 000

0
US$27 938 (30)

HDI (rank) 0 ———————— 1 **0.877** (12)

Internet access (rank) **81.6%** (11)

Mobile phone subscriptions per 100 people (rank) **100.7** (79)

All figures 2009

South Korea was formed by the partitioning of the Kingdom of Korea after the Second World War. Already devastated by Japanese occupation, the country's reconstruction was further hindered by the 1950–1953 Korean War, which ended in the stalemate that remains today. South Korea was ruled by a series of autocratic, military-dominated governments until 1987, when it moved to liberal democracy.

South Korea's full name is the Republic of Korea.

Since the 1960s South Korea has been one of the most successful economies in the world, regularly reporting yearly economic growth of over 6%. This success has been the result of economic planning, colossal investment and intense cooperation between government, citizens and private industry. The USA, keen to build a strong ally against Communist North Korea and China, financed much of the country's reconstruction as well as subsidising its defence, freeing up money for industrial growth. Like that of neighbouring Japan, the government of South Korea dictated the creation of particular industries, with exported goods a priority, and provided low-interest loans for industrial development. Trade barriers were raised against foreign imports. Economic development began with the establishment of steel and petrochemical industries, before moving to hi-tech products such as ships, cars and consumer electronics.

South Korea's largest companies are known as *chaebol* – conglomerates of many, often disparate, businesses trading under a single name. Some of these companies are well known in the West, including LG, Samsung and Daewoo. The chaebol proved to be willing partners in enacting government policies in exchange for finance, loan protection and guaranteed contracts.

Samsung is the most valuable multinational conglomerate in the world. Its 2009 revenues were US$119 billion.

Additionally, South Korea's development benefited from two national characteristics:

- Families saved a high percentage of their income, creating highly capitalised banks able to lend money for industrial development.

- There was a strong emphasis on education, both as government policy and amongst families. South Korea has some of the world's highest literacy and numeracy rates, which has meant a highly skilled workforce.

South Korea provides a good example of government, citizens and private industry working together. There are several advantages to this kind of approach to economic growth. For example, government funding makes large amounts of money available to businesses, which can make them more likely to succeed. On the other hand, companies might be overly dependent on government subsidies: if government policies change (for example, if a new government is elected) then the company might not survive.

Activity 12 (exploratory)

Try to think of another possible advantage and another possible disadvantage of the South Korean approach to industrial development.

Comment

I thought of the following advantages and disadvantages of the Korean model of development (there may be more).

Advantages

- Governments may be prepared to fund projects over the long term before they become commercially viable.

- Coordination allows industries to grow alongside the necessary infrastructure.

- Education and employment policies can be tailored to build a well-trained workforce.

- Competition within the economy can be reduced to ensure that companies are not battling one another.

Disadvantages

- There is a risk of corruption in the relationship between government and industry.

- Governments are not always responsive to the demands of consumers.

- There may be less scope for creativity and entrepreneurship within companies.

- Protecting domestic industry may mean that it is uncompetitive in the global market.

- World trade agreements do not approve of import barriers preventing foreign competition.

South Korea was once an isolated, ruined, poverty-stricken country; it is now an integral part of the world economy, a leading industrial and technological power.

South Korean communications

In 2009 the South Korean telecoms regulator, the Korean Communications Commission (KCC), reported that 94% of households had access to broadband internet services. Just as the South Korean government has fostered planned industrial development, the high level and speed of internet connectivity in the country is also the result of deliberate policy.

During the 1990s, the government eliminated a telecommunications monopoly held by Korea Telecom (KT). One of the first companies to enter the newly freed domestic market, Hanaro Telecom, decided not to compete with KT in voice communications, but instead to concentrate on the much less established market for broadband. Hanaro and others were given government protection from KT, which was initially forbidden to sell broadband connections. The fledgling internet industry was then given a boost by economic disaster. After decades of economic success, in 1997 Asian economies were hit hard by a financial crisis that in many ways presaged the economic problems of Europe and the USA from 2008 onwards. South Korea was one of the worst affected, with soaring unemployment, the possibility of civil unrest and many major companies at risk of bankruptcy. Faced with total economic collapse, the government dramatically changed industrial policy away from heavy industry and towards businesses based on computer and telecommunications technologies.

This transformation was made possible by the construction of a US$24 billion, nationwide, high-speed optical fibre network known as a 'fibre-to-the-home' (FTTH) system. With the enormous bandwidth of optical fibre, this is the very highest performance network currently possible. Alternative optical fibre networks found elsewhere in the world generally still use inefficient copper wiring to connect individual homes and offices. Table 5 lays out some of the possible options for optical fibre networks.

Table 5   Possible configurations for optical fibre networks

	Name	Description
Best	*Fibre-to-the-home (FTTH)* *Fibre-to-the-premises (FTTP)*	A network in which the optical fibre runs all the way to an individual home (FTTH) or office (FTTP). The internal network will use technologies such as Ethernet or wireless connections.
	Fibre-to-the-building (FTTB) – also known as *fibre-to-the-basement*	A network in which the optical fibre runs only as far as the boundary of a multi-tenanted building, with links to individual apartments or offices using alternative technologies.
	Fibre-to-the-cabinet (FTTC) – also known as *fibre-to-the-curb*	A network in which the optical fibre runs only as far as a street-side cabinet or under-pavement switch, with individual homes and offices being connected using copper wires no more than 300 m long.
Worst	*Fibre-to-the-node (FTTN)*	A network in which the optical fibre runs only as far as a street-side cabinet or small exchange, with the remainder of the network being connected using copper cables more than 300 m long.

Activity 13 (exploratory)

South Korea is a very densely populated, urban country, with many people living in modern high-density, high-rise apartment blocks. Why do you think it might have been easy to set up such an advanced network there, aside from the availability of money?

Comment

The high density of housing minimises the amount of cable needed to connect a large number of families. In fact, the buildings themselves have been designed to receive network cabling.

In 2009, the KCC announced that private telecoms companies and the Korean government would invest a further US$25 billion in modernising the network still further. Amongst its ambitions were the widespread deployment of 1 Gbps broadband to the home no later than 2012, and the creation of 120 000 new jobs.

> South Korea may have been slow to industrialize, but we will lead the world in computerization.
>
> A 1995 campaign slogan for the *Chosun Ilbo* newspaper's computer literacy promotion

By 2010, the speed of the average domestic broadband connection in South Korea was 20 Mbps, and in some specially designed 'cyber apartments' it was more than 100 Mbps. Not only was South Korea the most connected nation in the world, it also had the fastest average connection speeds.

Within Korea

Earlier, I claimed that digital divides may occur as much within nations as between them. Even an advanced nation such as South Korea has its own digital divide – between the well-connected urban masses and the outlying rural areas. As early as 1996, pilot projects were established to bring high-speed communications to distant regions. In 2001 the country passed the Digital Divide Act, which laid down *The First Master Plan on Bridging the Digital Divide*: a five-year, US$1.9 billion programme, the targets of which were to connect 10 000 schools to the internet and provide low-cost computers for poorer citizens. This has been followed by further, hugely expensive government programmes, *Cyber Korea 21* and the current *u-Korea Master Plan* (for ubiquitous computing).

In Session 3 I'll further consider digital divides within prosperous countries.

2.4   Estonia: leapfrogging the divide

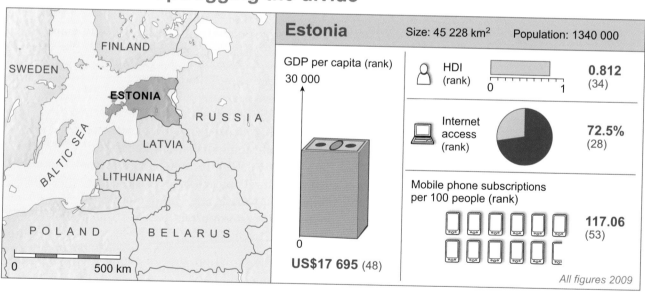

The Baltic state of Estonia first achieved independence from Russia following the First World War, but was annexed by the Soviet Union in 1939, only regaining full independence and converting to free-market economics in 1991. It became a member of the European Union in 2004.

Estonia's full name is the Republic of Estonia.

Note: the Soviet Union (USSR) was a Communist nation state founded in 1922 following the Russian Revolution and civil war that ended the Russian Empire. The Soviet Union was nominally composed of fifteen states, of which Russia was the largest member. After the collapse of Communism in 1991, the USSR's members became separate nations. Today Russia is an independent democratic republic.

Estonia was devastated by the Second World War and, although prosperous by the standards of the Soviet Union, Estonia's economy was backward in comparison to nearby Sweden and Finland. The collapse of Communist rule left the country with antiquated infrastructure and uncompetitive industries. If Estonia was to flourish, it would need to start almost from scratch. The new democratic government based its development strategy on Estonia's two strongest assets: its well-educated, multilingual and relatively cheap labour force, and its geographical position between the European Union and Russia. Its ambition was to turn Estonia into one of the five most developed nations in the European Union, by creating an economy based on financial services and high technology. Estonia hoped to follow the same process as the Republic of Ireland, which had transformed itself from one of Europe's poorest countries to one of its richest in under a generation.

The mobile economy

In 1991, when Estonia gained its independence, its communications infrastructure was as backward as its economy. Less than half the population had access to a private landline. The telephone network used archaic equipment, so calls were generally low-quality, unreliable and expensive. Today, Estonia is a leader in communications technology – but this has less to do with updating its fixed-line infrastructure than with building completely new mobile communications networks. By 2010 (the last year for which data was available), Estonia had gone from a country where telephones were rare, unreliable and expensive to one where there were more mobile phones than people, and where mobile communications were becoming an important part of social and economic life.

The graph in Figure 8 shows the growth in mobile phone adoption in the Baltic states of Estonia, Lithuania and Latvia, as well as in the neighbouring Russian Federation, Finland and Sweden. The UK is included for comparison. Note that some countries have more than 100 mobile phones per 100 people, meaning that some people own more than one mobile phone.

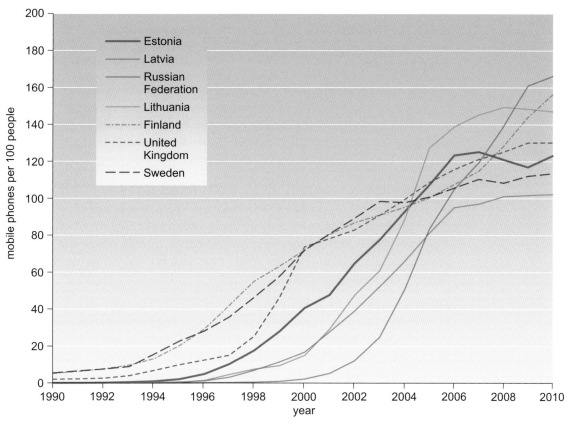

Figure 8   Growth in mobile phone adoption (the ex-Soviet republics of Estonia, Latvia, Lithuania and the Russian Federation are indicated by solid lines, whilst long-established Western countries are indicated by dashed lines)

Activity 14 (self-assessment)

Write a couple of paragraphs about what the graph in Figure 8 reveals about the take-up of mobile phones in Estonia, comparing and contrasting this with its Baltic neighbours and with the UK. Try to offer an explanation of some of the points you note.

By 2010 there were approximately 1.25 mobile phones for every Estonian, these being used to access a kaleidoscope of business and government services. Estonia has leapt from a primitive technological infrastructure to an advanced one in little over fifteen years. In part, this growth was made possible precisely because the existing infrastructure was so inadequate. It would have been possible to upgrade Estonia's fixed-line telephone network to equip every citizen with the latest technology, but this would have been an immensely disruptive and expensive undertaking. Roads and pavements would have been dug up, new exchanges would have been needed, and every home would have had to be connected – while at the same time keeping existing services running. By comparison, new mobile services could be supplied with little disruption, simply by building new base stations and linking to the existing fixed-line network using optical fibre.

Estonia built its mobile network with technological assistance and funding from Swedish and Finnish telecom companies, which were eager to attract new customers. Today the largest operator, EMT, retains these close links, as it is a joint company with Estonia's Eesti Telekom and the Swedish–Finnish consortium TeliaSonera AB.

The worldwide switch away from fixed lines

Estonia is not alone in moving towards a modern mobile telephony. UN statistics show that many countries currently undergoing rapid economic expansion are experiencing explosive growth in mobile phone use. At the same time, the market for fixed telephone lines is either growing relatively slowly or actually contracting.

The graphs in Figure 9 compare the growth in access to landline and mobile phones in ten nations that are undergoing rapid urbanisation and industrialisation. For contrast I have included South Korea, an industrialised country with well-established communications systems.

Activity 15 (exploratory)

Examine the two graphs shown in Figure 9 and write a set of bullet points summing up the points you notice.

Comment

Here are some of the points I noticed. In the graph of landline adoption:

- None of the countries have more than 60% adoption rates – lower than Western countries such as the USA (which peaked at 67% in 1999).
- There is a large gap between the percentage of people with fixed lines in South Korea and that in the other countries.
- Most countries have experienced slow rates of growth in fixed lines. In a number of them (e.g. South Korea, China and Turkey) the percentage of people with fixed lines has been falling, both as existing fixed-line subscribers switch to mobile phones and as new, young customers never choose a fixed-line connection.

In the graph of mobile phone adoption:

- South Korea was the first country to begin a rapid growth in mobile phone services.
- India not only has the lowest level of access to mobile phones but also has been the slowest to develop, although growth is accelerating.
- Several countries (Argentina, Malaysia and South Korea) are approaching or have exceeded 100% penetration.

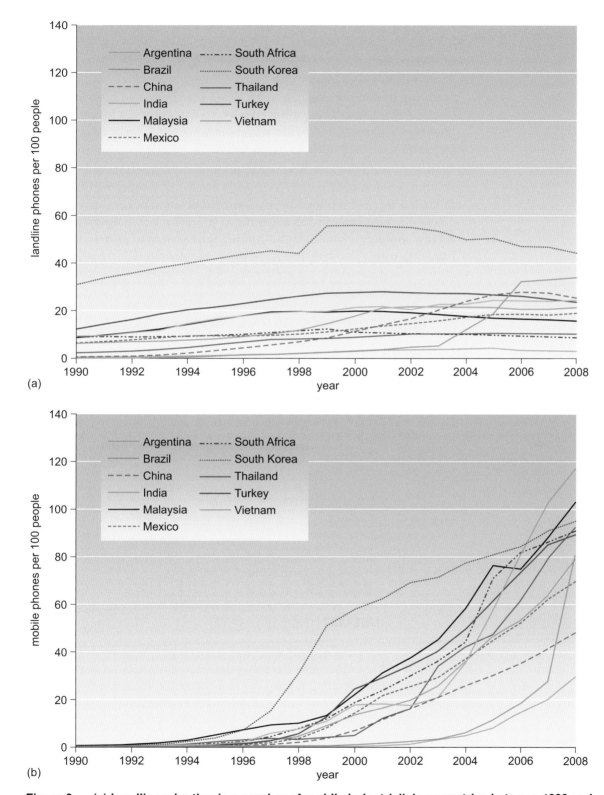

(a)

(b)

Figure 9   **(a) Landline adoption in a number of rapidly industrialising countries between 1990 and 2008; (b) adoption of mobile phones in the same countries over the same period**

Many of these trends can be explained by the political, geographical and economic circumstances of individual countries. To take just two examples:

- South Korea's high proportion of fixed lines is a result of the country's established economic success, high living standards and high levels of disposable income. These allowed telecom companies to invest in fixed lines many years ago. Additionally, South Korea's largely urban population is well suited to wired networks.

- Vietnam's sudden growth in fixed and mobile connections is a result of government policy. Vietnam's economic development is modelled on the highly successful industrialisation of neighbouring China; the government has encouraged private telecom operators to enter a competitive market and funded the creation of new infrastructure.

2.5 Bangladesh: village phones, kiosks and Infoladies

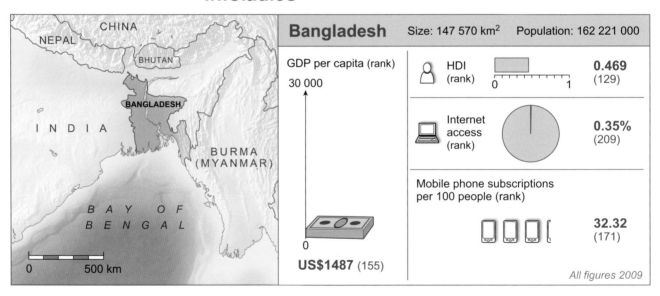

Bangladesh's full name is the People's Republic of Bangladesh.

Bangladesh is one of the most densely populated countries on Earth, with a large part of the population working in agriculture. Its economy has been growing steadily, with nearly three-quarters of earnings coming from the export of textiles and clothing to Western markets. Although over the last few years there has been considerable success in raising the living standards of much of Bangladesh's population, its HDI indicates that it remains amongst the world's poorest nations. Development has been hampered by relatively low levels of literacy, poor infrastructure, endemic corruption and lack of access to education and technology.

Nevertheless, Bangladesh has produced a number of revolutionary projects that have achieved genuine success in lifting people out of extreme poverty. Many of these originated within the country from local entrepreneurs familiar with its society. Fundamental to this approach has been the Grameen Bank.

The Grameen Bank

Small businesses are one of the best ways of raising people out of poverty, but their development is hampered by the refusal of traditional banks to extend credit to people on low incomes or without assets.

The Grameen Bank, awarded the Nobel Peace Prize in 2006, is a provider of *microcredit*: it lends relatively small sums of money without security to individuals or groups in order to establish businesses, and offers small interest-free loans to the poorest for necessities such as mosquito nets. The bank was founded in 1976 by the Bangladeshi economist Muhammad Yunus. That year Yunus lent US$27 to a group of extremely poor rural families making bamboo furniture so that they could buy raw materials. Previously the community had only had access to credit through moneylenders, who charged very high rates of interest that had to be repaid from any profits, leaving little for the workers. Yunus' loan was repaid; the group made a tiny profit and were able to break free of the moneylenders.

Similar pilot projects showed that microcredit had the potential to raise millions of people out of extreme poverty. Their success persuaded the Bangladeshi government to offer its own loan to Yunus' organisation, which became the Grameen Bank in 1979. Today the Grameen Bank operates in more than 40 countries and employs some 25 000 people.

By the end of 2009 the Grameen Bank had lent approximately US$8.75 billion to its eight million members, with an average business loan being less than US$350. Of the bank's members, 97% are women – extraordinary in a society where women have not traditionally managed their own finances. The bank claims that more than 98% of loans are fully repaid, although some economists dispute this figure.

The Grameen Bank has a presence in almost every town and village in Bangladesh. As well as providing financial help to the poor, the bank encourages family planning, education and efficient farming. Some of its most significant work has been in developing communications within Bangladesh.

The Village Phone programme

Grameen Bank's Village Phone programme brings basic telephony to people who are too poor to afford a handset or even the cheapest

This programme is not related to the South African Village Phone scheme mentioned earlier.

mobile phone services. The scheme provides an individual with a US$200 loan to buy a mobile phone on a contract with Grameen Telecom, a not-for-profit telecom operator offering relatively cheap calls and other mobile services.

Like Grameen Bank's microcredit, the phone service has proved especially popular with women, who have used Village Phone to dramatically improve their standard of living by lending their phone to others, charging them only for making and receiving calls and sending messages (Figure 10). This money is used to gradually repay the bank loan. In 1997, there were just 32 Village Phones in Bangladesh; twelve years later there were more than 362 000 in 50 000 villages (Grameen Foundation, n.d.). The Village Phone idea has been exported to other developing nations including Uganda (Figure 11), Rwanda and Indonesia.

Figure 10   A customer making a call at 'Nomita Telecom', the phone booth of a Grameen Village Phone owner

Figure 11   Josephine Namala, a shop owner in Lukonda, Uganda, celebrates after becoming one of Grameen's Village Phone operators

However, the long-term viability of the Village Phone programme is uncertain, with potentially serious consequences for those people who own the phones. The problems facing Village Phone inside Bangladesh are twofold:

1   Many villages now have more than one Village Phone, and even in those villages where there is only a single owner there are rival services nearby. Competition has led to cutthroat pricing, some of which is uneconomic.

2   As the price of handsets falls and coverage improves, mobile phones are becoming an appealing alternative to the Village Phone. Between 1995 and 2007, the price of a low-end mobile phone in Bangladesh fell by more than 90% to just US$22, whilst ownership grew 60-fold. Ironically, it has been Grameen's own mobile telephone operator, Grameenphone, that has been the major driver in reducing the cost of mobile connections inside Bangladesh.

Village Phone will probably remain viable only as long as other phones – fixed-line or mobile – remain scarce. Average Village Phone income peaked in 2003, with a typical owner bringing in US$917. Three years later this had fallen to just US$396. In Bangladesh, the Village Phone might now be a technology that has served its purpose and been replaced by better ones. The future for those who participated in the original scheme is uncertain. One possibility is that they will move on to Grameen Telecom's next project – the kiosk.

Activity 16 (self-assessment)

Explain briefly the characteristics of Village Phone that make it an appropriate technology.

Community kiosks

Grameen Telecom's most ambitious rural development programme is to provide internet access to villages through information 'kiosks'. These can be sited in offices, shops or even homes, and contain one or more internet-enabled PCs equipped with printers, scanners and webcams. Typical kiosk services include email, web browsing, VoIP phone calls and video-conferencing services.

The relatively high cost of a kiosk requires that it is owned by a community or by a group of entrepreneurs (again, a significant number of these are women) who obtain a loan from Grameen Bank to buy the equipment and services. The owners of the kiosk are trained to maintain it by Grameen Telecom, who also provide basic training to users, along with ongoing support from the operator's central staff. By 2010, more than 500 community kiosks were operating across Bangladesh.

Infoladies

The Development Research Network (D.Net) is a Bangladeshi non-profit organisation dedicated to developing the country's economy through information technology. Among its projects is a scheme to recruit women as technology ambassadors – the so-called Infoladies.

Infoladies travel from village to village, often by bicycle, bringing telecommunications and basic information to the remotest communities. Each Infolady is provided with a netbook computer, a mobile phone to act as a modem, a telephone headset, a webcam, a digital camera and a small photo printer. They may also travel with pregnancy testing kits and blood pressure monitors to perform routine medical check-ups. Their computers are pre-loaded with Bangla language information ranging from material on basic medical care to relevant legal and agricultural advice. Thus Bangladeshi villagers can seek help from an Infolady without knowing anything about computers: she presents information to them on screen in the form of simple text, pictures and animations (Figure 12). If a problem requires professional advice, the Infolady can either make a telephone call to one of a number of dedicated helplines or take photographs and email them for expert analysis.

> She matched the picture of my crop with the one on her TV [netbook] and recommended a certain pesticide. I haven't had problems since.
>
> Nahar Hossain, rice farmer

> Ask me about the pest that's infecting your crop, common skin diseases, how to seek help if your husband beats you or even how to stop having children, and I may have a solution.
>
> Luich Akhter, an Infolady
>
> Both quoted in Kumar (2009)

Figure 12   An Infolady gives advice

Once again, the participation of women has proved crucial. The Infoladies have turned out to be more than a source of technical advice; they have become confidantes of women seeking gynaecological, contraceptive and legal advice in a society with strictly enforced religious and social structures. Not only have they become extremely popular and useful, but they are also highlighting serious issues that should be addressed by government, such as the rights of women, access to contraception and law enforcement.

> I inform them about their rights and warn their husbands they could go to jail.
>
> Luich Akhter

> She is a terror – the men are scared of her; even the clerics fear her.
>
> Najma Begum, manager of the telecentre in Chandipur

> After 6pm I change my SIM as I get calls from angry or besotted men. They are scared of me in the daylight, but they all want to marry me after six.
>
> Luich Akhter
>
> All quoted in Kumar (2009)

2.6 The digital divide: comparing solutions

In this session you have looked at case studies that demonstrate four distinct strategies for introducing the modern communications technologies that are fundamental in bridging the digital divide between poorer countries and the prosperous West. But why were these strategies so different from one another, and why have they led to such different results so far?

Perhaps the most obvious reason is that the four different countries all started in quite different circumstances. Although all of them began in relative poverty and with poor infrastructure, in most other ways they were vastly different. Specifically, we might point to four overlapping areas of variation:

1   *Politics*. Each country had its own political set-up, and a government that made specific choices.

2   *Population*. The populations of the four countries I've discussed had distinct characteristics – ethnic, cultural, educational and so on. Populations also varied from largely urban to largely rural.

3   *Economics*. The four countries had dissimilar economies: rural, industrial, etc.

4   *Geography*. Each country had a different size, geographical location, nature (of the land) and climate, and its neighbouring countries were also vastly different.

Now let's try to examine this in a little more detail.

Activity 17 (exploratory)

Table 6 lays out the factors I've just identified. For each country, write a few notes in the appropriate space about that country's starting circumstances. To help you, I've included a sample entry for South Africa. If you feel there is not enough information in the case studies then refer to Wikipedia or some other knowledge source.

Table 6 Areas of variation in the four case studies

Country	Politics	Population	Economics	Geography
South Africa	Relatively stable. Full democracy since 1994.	Well-educated, skilled elite with poorly educated masses. Low HDI.	Mixed agricultural and industrial. Relatively poor infrastructure outside towns.	Mixed – rural with large urban centres.
South Korea				
Estonia				
Bangladesh				

Comment

Table 7 lists some suggested points.

Table 7 Areas of variation in the four case studies (completed)

Country	Politics	Population	Economics	Geography
South Africa	Relatively stable. Full democracy since 1994.	Well-educated, skilled elite with poorly educated masses. Low HDI.	Mixed agricultural and industrial. Relatively poor infrastructure outside towns.	Mixed – rural with large urban centres.
South Korea	Stable democracy since 1987. Industry and government work closely together.	Highly skilled and well educated. Very high HDI.	Industrial.	Mainly urban with some poorly served outlying areas. Unstable northern neighbour.
Estonia	Stable democracy since 1991. Some ethnic tensions.	Skilled and well educated. High HDI.	Mainly industrial.	Mainly urban. Close ties with neighbouring prosperous democracies.
Bangladesh	Democracy with some corruption, political violence and terrorism.	Generally poorly skilled with low literacy levels. Densely populated. Very low HDI.	Mainly agricultural with some industry.	Mainly rural, with few urban centres.

There are plenty of other possible observations that you could have made.

So the path a nation chooses to take towards bridging the digital divide is bound to depend on where it starts from, and this is clearly dependent on a multitude of factors – economic, cultural, historical and political. But equally, there is no single road to the goal of the digital society. Despite what many commentators seem to believe, merely having a good communications infrastructure in place is no guarantee of a happy and prosperous future.

2.7 Conclusion

In this session you saw how four very different countries are bridging the digital divide. You learned about the concept of appropriate technology, and applied that concept in different contexts.

You have seen from the case studies in this session that the ways in which a country chooses to *use* ICTs are also many and various. I will look in a little more detail at these in Session 4. In addition, Session 5 will present a further case study, guiding you to find out more information about it for yourself.

You have also learned that even the most prosperous nations may harbour digital divides within themselves. I will examine this issue in more detail in the next session.

This session should have helped you with the following learning outcomes.

- Describe the concept of a digital divide and some of its different aspects.
- Describe the different scales of the digital divide (local, national and global).
- Describe approaches to technological development in a number of different countries and explain the reasons for these approaches.
- Describe the roles of government, private industry, communities and individuals in bridging the digital divide.
- Describe some of the social, political and economic factors influencing the digital divide.
- Analyse examples of appropriate technology in the context of the digital divide.

3 The digital divide: within nations

The common understanding of the digital divide is that it is a gulf between the use of information technology in developed nations and its use in developing nations without widespread access to computers and communications. But as I argued in Session 1, even very prosperous nations can have digital divides within them. In this short session I will explore this idea further.

3.1 Digital USA

Even in the most technologically sophisticated countries, such as South Korea and the USA, there may still be huge internal differences in ICT access and skills between, for example:

- urban and rural areas
- economic classes
- age groups
- educational levels
- genders
- ethnic groups
- recent immigrants and more established communities.

The largest surveys of the digital divides within a country have been conducted by the US National Telecommunications & Information Administration (NTIA). Its *Falling through the Net* studies are unparalleled in the number of participants and the detail of questioning. The last of the NTIA's reports was delivered in the late 1990s, but it uncovered some uncomfortable truths about US citizens' levels of access to computer technologies. One striking statistical graphic taken from the report is shown in Figure 13.

Activity 18 (exploratory)

Note down a few aspects of the digital divide in the USA, as revealed by the chart in Figure 13.

Comment

Here are a few points I noted:

1   Computer access is strongly positively correlated with income across all ethnic groups.

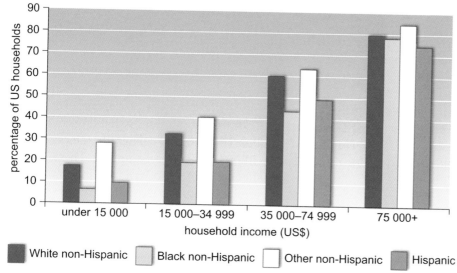

Figure 13   Percentage of US households with a computer in 1998, by income and ethnicity (redrawn from NTIA, 1999)

2   White people and non-Hispanic others have generally higher computer access than black and Hispanic people.

3   Black people have the lowest levels of computer access in all but the top income group.

4   In the top income group, the disparities in levels of access between ethnic groups are much smaller than those for people on lower incomes.

These findings support the point I made in Session 1 about the correlation of digital access with wealth.

Digital divides based on education and geography were also apparent in the survey:

•   A person with a college degree or higher was more than 8 times more likely to have a home computer and 16 times more likely to have internet access than someone with only an elementary school education.

•   A high-income urban family was 20 times more likely to have internet access than a low-income rural family.

Participation in digital technologies is rising amongst all sectors of the populations of most nations, developed or otherwise, but the trend is not uniform. Some groups adopt new technologies more readily than others; even within individual families there are likely to be differences. Perhaps you are the trendsetter in your family, or maybe the laggard?

3.2 Digital UK

Every ranking of communications access shows the UK to be among the most connected countries in the world. But the UK, too, has its digital divides, some of them severe enough to prompt government action. In 2008, the Department for Communities and Local Government published a report called *Delivering Digital Inclusion: An Action Plan for Consultation* (HM Government, 2008) that highlighted what is sometimes called the *Final Third*: the 17 million UK citizens – generally the poor, elderly and ethnic minorities – without access to a computer. These citizens are excluded from crucial benefits of a modern information society, especially news and government services. And it can be precisely the poor, elderly and minority citizens who have most need of government services.

Activity 19 (exploratory)

The *Delivering Digital Inclusion* document was intended to inform government policy and promote wider discussion on the topic of the digital divide. Use the link in the resources page associated with this part on the TU100 website to download a copy of the report.

(a) Chapter Two lists a number of sectors of the population and how digital technologies apply to them. For each sector, list the advantages of wider digital inclusion.

   Do you feel that any of the points especially apply to you? Or can you identify a need of your own (whether for personal, family or career purposes) to which digital technologies are well suited?

(b) Point 15 of Chapter Three (page 28) contains a list of factors that can increase digital exclusion. Do any of these factors (there may be more than one) apply to you or to a member of your family? If so, describe briefly how this factor causes you difficulty and how you attempt to overcome it. If not, then think of someone you know or have heard of to whom a factor applies, and explain how it affects them.

Comment

Below are my notes on the advantages of digital inclusion for different sectors of the population.

Young people
*   Achieving potential, both academic and personal, by using ICTs to access information, develop skills and address different learning styles.

Adults

- Gaining and maintaining employment.
- Balancing work, family and other responsibilities.
- Accessing online services and information.
- For those with disabilities, accessing assistive technologies.
- Reducing reoffending rates amongst prisoners.

Older people

- Maintaining independent living through telecare.
- Maintaining paid or unpaid employment.
- Reducing social isolation.
- Accessing goods and services.

Communities

- Enabling communities to be heard.
- Reducing isolation.
- Reducing negative human impact on the environment.

Your notes will be different, but I hope you made similar points. The rest of your response to this activity will be personal to you.

The digital champion

The UK government considered the problem of digital exclusion so pressing that in 2009 it appointed Martha Lane Fox, co-founder of lastminute.com, to the two-year post of Champion for Digital Inclusion. Her role was to represent the Final Third in discussions with government departments and private companies.

> I don't think you can be a proper citizen of our society in the future if you are not engaged online.
>
> Martha Lane Fox, quoted in Bowlby (2009)

You were first introduced to the post of 'Champion for Digital Inclusion' in Block 5 Part 1.

Following a change of government in 2010, the role was redefined to emphasise community action and private investment. The promotion of greater access was placed under the banner of 'Race Online 2012', a hub where businesses, charities and individuals could share their resources and skills. Race Online was deliberately set up to address the problem of digital exclusion at a national and a local level, with top-level initiatives backed by large companies working alongside local activities targeting particular communities. Race Online aimed to reassure people about every aspect of getting online: from buying a computer to accessing the internet and learning how to use it.

In association with BT and Microsoft, Get Online @ Home offered low-cost internet-ready computers for just £165 (£95 for people receiving certain benefits and to charities) including delivery, setup and technical support. Mobile broadband support was also offered for just £10 per month, undercutting most commercial services.

As you are no doubt aware, getting online is only the beginning, so Race Online 2012 sought to create tens of thousands of digital champions who would act to inspire new computer users, help set up equipment for others, act as informal technical support, provide training and offer unwanted equipment to other users. Digital champions could be private citizens or volunteer to act in the role for their company. Alongside many other employers, The Open University publicised the role of digital champions amongst its staff and students. One of the biggest promotions of digital champions took place in October 2011 to coincide with the end of British Summer Time. Individuals were encouraged to give one hour of their time to demonstrating the benefits of the World Wide Web to people who had never been online. The campaign was backed by the BBC, publishing companies and the Scouts, and run through JobCentrePlus employment bureaux, local libraries, schools and mobile phone shops.

Activity 20 (exploratory)

Shortly after her appointment in 2009, Martha Lane Fox was interviewed about her role as Champion for Digital Inclusion by the BBC's economics correspondent Robert Peston. In the resources page associated with this part on the TU100 website you will find a video clip that lets you hear her own opinion on the challenge of narrowing the digital divide.

Connecting the countryside

Although governments are clear that rural areas benefit from the introduction of high-speed digital services, the question is whether it is economic to offer them. Since the 1980s, most countries have either partly or fully privatised their telecommunications industries, meaning that services are now provided on purely economic grounds. Companies thus prefer to concentrate on serving urban populations, because communications technologies are most cost-effective in densely populated cities, where large numbers of people can be served by short cables and a few base stations. Remote areas need large amounts of cabling, or expensive long-distance wireless technologies (see Box 4) that may never recoup the initial investment.

Box 4 Long-distance wireless

A number of wireless technologies can be used where wired connections are impossible.

- The most common links rely on the same *cellular networks* as mobile phones.

- An alternative that is rapidly growing in use is *WiMAX* (officially known as the IEEE 802.16 standard), which can transmit data up to 50 km from a base station, although the speed of any connection drops as distance increases.

- Finally, very remote areas can send and receive data through links to a number of communications satellites. As you might expect, these *satellite links* are comparatively expensive and are generally not affordable by domestic users even in developed countries.

The result has been a digital divide between those who can access high-speed internet (mostly city-dwellers) and those who cannot (mostly rural citizens). The phenomenon has become so widespread that rural areas with little or no connectivity have been christened *not spots*.

Activity 21 (exploratory)

This activity asks you to help me plot internet speeds across the UK. On the resources page for this part you will find a link to a broadband speed checker and a form to submit your results. Follow the instructions on the speed check site to obtain your download and upload speeds, then fill out the form to add your results to the survey. Once you have done this, view the cumulative results for students across TU100. What patterns can you spot? Is your result typical for your area? (If you are one of the first students to submit your data then come back later on.)

If you are not in the UK then you don't need to add any results to the survey, but take a look at other students' results to see if you can spot any patterns.

The Rural Broadband Initiative

In 2009, the Labour government responded to *Delivering Digital Inclusion* with the Rural Broadband Initiative (RBI): a plan to deliver, by no later than 2012, at least 2 Mbps broadband to every address in the UK, using fibre optics, microwave and satellite. Given its price tag of £3 billion, there was understandable reluctance to fund RBI from taxation. Instead, some £250 million was to be diverted from existing funds set aside for helping people switch to digital television. The remainder of the sum would be gradually recovered through a monthly levy of 50p on every UK landline.

The RBI never became law. The plan was dropped during the passing of the Digital Economy Bill of 2010. Following the 2010 general election, the new coalition government abandoned the 2012 deadline, instead promising to offer 2 Mbps access to everyone in the country by 2015.

Closing the Cornish digital divide

Despite its reputation as a holiday destination for the wealthy, Cornwall is the poorest county in England. Its industries – mineral extraction, dairy farming and fishing – are all in long-term decline. Many well-paid jobs have been lost, the county has suffered a 'brain drain' and its economy is now heavily dependent on unskilled, low-paid, often seasonal work. Cornwall also suffers from relatively poor infrastructure and inadequate communications; as a result, its economy lags far behind that of neighbouring Devon.

Cornwall's difficulties attracted funding from the European Union's Objective One programme – a scheme in which European and national money is directed to areas where the mean income is 75% or less than the European mean. Between 2000 and 2007, £300 million from the European Union – and a matching sum from the UK government – was pumped into Cornwall to improve infrastructure, train the workforce and increase employment.

Objective One targeted ten areas of the economy (known as 'clusters') for investment. Two of these, 'Digital Infrastructure' and 'The Knowledge Economy', were directly aimed at narrowing aspects of the digital divide in Cornwall. During the project, many telephone exchanges in the county were upgraded to provide ADSL broadband connections ahead of those in more wealthy regions of the UK. Alongside the technological improvements to the county's infrastructure, a non-profit organisation called *actnow* was set up to raise awareness of broadband and assist with connections. It is quite remarkable how pedestrian many of the actnow projects seem today, but as little as a decade ago it was rare for farmers to have up-to-the-minute continuous weather forecasting, for small businesses to have their own online shops or for hotels to accept reservations over the internet.

Beyond Objective One, in 2010 a consortium consisting of BT and the European Union announced plans to bring ultra-high-speed broadband to more than 90% of properties in Cornwall by the end of 2014. The £131 million scheme plans to connect most properties using either FTTP or FTTC fibre-optic connections. More remote properties will be linked to the main network using very high-speed long-distance wireless connections. Figure 14 shows the chief executive of BT, Ian Livingston, and the Leader

Up-to-date information on progress towards this aim is available on the part resources page.

'Brain drain' is a term used for the emigration of skilled or highly educated workers from a particular area, often because there are better-paid jobs available elsewhere.

Figure 14   Ian Livingston (left) and Alec Robertson launch the plan to offer fibre connections across Cornwall

of Cornwall Council, Alec Robertson, launching the plan at Fistral Beach, Newquay.

3.3   Who is helping to bridge the digital divide?

In this section you will take part in developing an internet directory of organisations, companies and groups that address issues relating to the digital divide. I am interested in everything that is going on, so topics might include computer literacy programmes, cheap computers, training for the elderly or disabled, involvement with religious or ethnic groups, help with setting up computers or networks, employment advice, sites offering free internet access, etc.

Activity 22 (exploratory)

I would like you to add information to the collaborative database that I have set up for this part. Start by looking for initiatives reported in your local press. Alternatively, you might look for offerings in areas that especially interest you – particular age groups, single-parent families, minority groups, disabled people, service personnel and their families, ex-offenders and so on. There are many groups addressing these issues.

Next, choose one such initiative and add it to the database using the form provided. You will be asked to supply information about the initiative including its name, a description and a web address. Make your entry as detailed and as accurate as you can so that it is helpful to other users of the database.

Finally, you may like to search the database for further initiatives in the area that you are interested in.

3.4   Conclusion

In this short session you have learned that digital divides still exist even inside countries as wealthy as the USA and the UK.

You looked at a number of UK government initiatives to address problems of access. These appear to have had limited effectiveness, not least because policies change faster than the projects can be expected to deliver. Often these policy shifts stem from deep-rooted differences in political philosophy: a Labour government choosing to fund infrastructure improvements through a compulsory levy, the Conservative–Liberal Democrat coalition government preferring individual, community and private investment. However, you also saw how a combination of

European, national and private enterprise has made significant inroads into closing the digital divide in Cornwall.

This session should have helped you with the following learning outcomes.

- Describe the concept of a digital divide and some of its different aspects.
- Describe the different scales of the digital divide (local, national and global).
- Describe approaches to technological development in a number of different countries and explain the reasons for these approaches.
- Describe the roles of government, private industry, communities and individuals in bridging the digital divide.
- Explain the importance of the digital divide in relation to other divides (e.g. cultural, political, economic, etc.).
- Describe some of the social, political and economic factors influencing the digital divide.

Why bridge the divide?

4

To read the views of some commentators, you would think that all that's necessary to guarantee the future prosperity, stability and happiness of a nation is for it to acquire high-speed digital information and communications technology – connect the people up and utopia will follow automatically. And as you learned in Session 1, national wealth is strongly correlated with access to information technology, so there may be some truth in this idea.

We can probably agree that making it easier for people to speak to each other and access information is a good thing. But the economic development and relative wellbeing of a nation is a hugely complex phenomenon, dependent on countless historical, geographical, demographic, political, social and cultural factors. Introducing ICTs must surely be only a first step on any nation's road to prosperity. It's what you do with them that matters.

So let's continue the discussion by revisiting the four digital case studies from Session 2 and looking a little more closely at the uses that have been made of ICTs in each country.

4.1   Africa

One of the most dynamic telecommunications markets in Africa is Kenya, which lies on Africa's eastern equatorial coast. The country has been a relatively stable democracy since obtaining independence from the UK. Kenya is experiencing rapid population growth and urbanisation, which have placed strains on the country's society and its economy. Although Kenya has sometimes struggled to raise living standards, its indigenous ICT industry has proved to be especially successful – a number of home-developed businesses have revolutionised aspects of Kenyan life and are now being exported around the world.

Mobile banking
More than 94% of UK citizens have at least one bank account; only 29% of Kenyans do. There is an enormous demand for banking across Africa, but African banks generally serve a wealthy elite. Many are poorly managed, under-capitalised and impose high charges, especially for money transfer.

Money transfer is vital in many communities where members of a family work elsewhere. Africa's rapid economic growth has led to mass movements of labour, both from the countryside to the cities and from country to country. Much of the movement is undocumented, so the number of migrant workers in Africa is unknown – but it is certainly in the tens of millions. Most migrants expect to send much of their salary back to families, but traditional banking services – even when available – are poorly suited to a low-paid, rootless, mobile labour force.

This gap is being filled by *mobile banking* (or *M-banking*), in which services are provided through a mobile phone. When it was first promoted in the West in the middle of the 1990s, mobile banking was soon supplanted by more efficient internet banking. However, where the alternative is either no bank at all or very expensive services, mobile banking has been a revolution.

M-PESA's name is from the Swahili for money, 'pesa' – the 'M' meaning 'mobile'.

In mid-2011 there were approximately 150 Kenyan shillings to the pound sterling.

The most well-established mobile banking network in Africa is M-PESA, operated by the Kenyan mobile phone network Safaricom and developed as the result of a collaboration between Safaricom, Vodafone, the UK's Department for International Development (DFID) and Sagentia, a Cambridge-based technology consulting company. M-PESA allows registered Safaricom customers to credit, transfer, receive or withdraw between 100 and 35 000 Kenyan shillings without visiting a bank or ATM; unregistered customers can only receive money from registered M-PESA users. All M-PESA transactions are completed within minutes, no matter where or when they are made. Crucially, money can be sent to anyone who owns a mobile phone.

Money is deposited with and withdrawn from M-PESA through a network of agents (Figure 15) – often established traders such as those who run supermarkets, market stalls, cyber cafés, village stores and petrol stations, who are already commercially trained and have access to cash, banking services and security. In a country where corruption is rife, the agents have a reputation for fairness in their communities. The agents' own income comes from a commission paid by the recipient of the payment, which is paid into the agent's own M-PESA account. Whilst M-PESA cannot offer free banking, it is much cheaper than using a traditional bank; it is also well suited to low-value transactions.

Figure 15   Making an M-PESA payment through an agent

Transfers between customers are conducted entirely through mobile phones without the intervention of an agent. The sender selects 'Send money' on their phone, then enters the phone number of the recipient, the amount of money to be sent and their PIN. As soon as transfer is complete, the recipient receives a text message informing them that their account has been credited.

Activity 23 (self-assessment)

Which aspects of M-PESA make it an appropriate technology?

M-PESA was founded in 2007. Its first year of operation in Kenya attracted over two million clients, who used the service to transfer more than £145 million. Two years later, in October 2009, there were more than six million active users, who exchanged some £80 million that month alone. By 2010, there were more than eleven thousand M-PESA agents throughout Kenya (slightly more than the number of bank branches in the UK). Kenya's established banks forced the Central Bank of Kenya to investigate M-PESA's financial stability in 2008, but this was popularly seen as a cynical attempt to undermine a competitor. The investigation concluded that M-PESA was financially sound, was well managed and should continue operating.

M-PESA now operates in Tanzania, South Africa, Egypt and India. Under the name M-Paisa, it is also bringing banking services to much of Afghanistan. Competing mobile banking services run by other mobile operators, such as South Africa's MTN, have been launched across Africa.

LIFELINK in Kenya

Ever-increasing demands for power, clean water and sewerage from a rapidly expanding population often outstrip what can be provided. Kenya's water supply is also under pressure as a result of the diversion of water for commercial agriculture and industry, whilst the country is both vulnerable to drought and experiencing a long-term decline in rainfall. Millions of Kenyans have no reliable, clean source of water. To try and ease their plight, Safaricom has joined the Danish pump manufacturer Grundfos to develop the LIFELINK solar-powered water pump for rural areas (Figure 16a). The pump delivers a fixed amount of clean water in exchange for a small payment made from a smartcard or RFID key fob (Figure 16b), loaded with credit from a user's M-PESA account. The community pays no upfront fee for the equipment; instead the pump's cost is repaid through a small charge on top of every transaction. The same wireless network that handles payments also transmits diagnostic information, allowing faulty pumps to be fixed quickly.

(a)

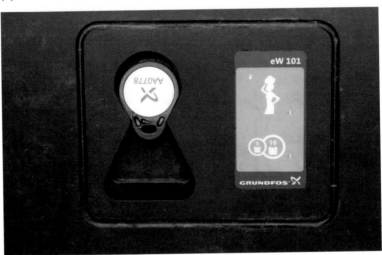

(b)

Figure 16   The Grundfos LIFELINK water pump: (a) typical installation in rural Kenya (the solar panels are on top of the large storage tank); (b) close-up of the controls where users place a smartcard or RFID key fob

Africa Unsigned

Africa has a vibrant musical culture that is largely unknown to most of the world. What little music does reach Europe and the USA is categorised as 'world music' and is not heavily promoted, remaining very much a niche product. Even inside Africa, distribution and promotion is patchy.

Africa Unsigned (Figure 17) is a European/African collaboration using Web 2.0 technology to raise awareness of African music and to fund new artists. It was founded in 2009 by the Dutch businessman Pim Betist, whose earlier online venture, SellaBand, had launched a number of artists by obtaining small donations from fans. The concept of Africa Unsigned is simple: agents across Africa locate new artists and pass their work to an expert panel for assessment. Once an artist is selected for inclusion then recordings, a profile and their details are uploaded onto the Africa Unsigned website, hosted in Amsterdam.

Figure 17   The Africa Unsigned home page in 2011

Activity 24 (self-assessment)

An obvious reason for using a site hosted in the Netherlands is that Africa Unsigned was founded by a Dutch company. Can you think of another reason for using a site hosted in the Netherlands?

Visitors to the site can browse through charts, search for music that matches their taste and listen to reasonably high-quality versions of any track for free. If a listener particularly likes an artist then they can support that artist by donating any amount from US$1 upwards. If an artist attracts US$10 000 in sponsorship, the site will arrange for professional studio recording of their work, which will then be sold across Africa and Europe on conventional record labels and on iTunes and Amazon. Supporters receive free digital copies of their artists' recordings, and profit from their success – half the proceeds of any sale go to the artist, while the remainder is divided between the artist's supporters according to their contribution.

Activity 25 (exploratory)

Spend no more than five minutes browsing the Africa Unsigned site, a link to which is available in the resources page for this part. Try to find out the name of the funding model employed. What are the benefits of this model for (a) the artist and (b) their supporters?

Comment

The funding model is known as crowd funding.

The benefit for the artist is that they may be able to raise the funds needed to access an expensive recording studio, where they can produce the high-quality recordings required by professional labels. An additional benefit of Africa Unsigned is that it brings the artist to a large potential audience. The benefits for the supporters are that they can directly contribute to the success of their preferred artist, obtain recordings at relatively low cost, and potentially share the profits if their artists become successful.

One Laptop Per Child

Although it was not specifically an African initiative, One Laptop Per Child (OLPC) – the brainchild of Professor Nicholas Negroponte – has been deployed in Ethiopia, Ghana, Rwanda and Sierra Leone. Negroponte was one of the founders of the influential *Wired* magazine, and of MIT's Media Lab, which has spawned technologies ranging from robotics to computer graphics and smart toys. After leaving the Media Lab, Negroponte devoted his efforts to bringing computer technology to the developing world.

Negroponte's vision was simple: cheap computers could bring education and business opportunities to millions. Yet computers were designed almost entirely with Western customers in mind; their real benefits would be felt only if everyone had access to one. *Everyone* included children, the theory being that developing the skills and confidence to use ICTs was best achieved by starting in childhood, and that these skills would give people opportunities that would allow them to escape poverty. A machine capable of satisfying the requirements of the developing world would have to be:

- cheap enough to be affordable even in very poor countries

- powerful enough to run modern applications, including word processors and drawing programs, and to browse the Web

- free from expensive software licences

- power-efficient enough to run for a reasonable length of time without mains electricity

- tough enough to survive being handled by a child, or in dirty or dusty conditions.

A few existing laptops met some of these requirements, but none at an acceptable cost. A completely new machine was required, and its inspiration came from the very first laptop of all – Alan Kay's Dynabook.

Activity 26 (exploratory)

You first encountered the OLPC XO-1 in Block 2 Part 2, where you saw how this small, cheap laptop closely corresponds to Alan Kay's vision of the Dynabook. In the resources page associated with this part on the TU100 website, you will find an interview with Kay in which he talks about OLPC and the design of the XO-1 laptop. Even if you chose to watch this video in Block 2 Part 2, it would be worth refreshing your memory here.

The idea of releasing a 'one-hundred-dollar laptop' proved to be too ambitious: the XO-1 was unveiled in 2007 at US$199, in the hope that mass production and cheaper components would eventually push the price towards the US$100 mark. The XO-1 was only available to partners in the OLPC who were prepared to buy it in large numbers. At first this meant only governments or state education authorities, but in 2007 OLPC ran the first of several 'gift one, get one' schemes, where for US$398 Western customers could buy one XO-1 for themselves and pay for a second to be donated to an OLPC partner.

By 2011, nearly two million XO-1s had been ordered by educational institutions or governments in seventeen countries. South America had been the most enthusiastic adopter of the technology: Uruguay was the first country to order 100 000 computers, followed by a further 200 000 so that every schoolchild between the age of six and twelve would have their own computer. Poorer countries, including Haiti and Mongolia, were the recipients of thousands more machines donated by the 'gift one, get one' schemes.

Superficially, OLPC has been a huge success – but as you will see later, the scheme is not without its critics.

4.2 South Korea

As you learned in Session 2, South Korea has grown from being poor and isolated into one of the most developed and highly connected countries in the world. South Korea is now home to several major electronics manufacturers, including LG and Samsung. These companies have been attempting to shake off a perception that they are cheap copycats of Western and Japanese brands by demonstrating technologies not offered by their better-known rivals. The idea of a smart, internet-connected domestic appliance is one example.

Smart appliances

Our vision is to create appliances that go beyond a simple mechanical function, like heating food or keeping it cold. Instead, these next-generation appliances will perform greater tasks, such as collecting recipes, preparing meals and keeping pantries stocked – tasks that require intelligence.

Simon Kang, President, LG Electronics, U.S.A., Inc., speaking at the US launch of the internet refrigerator

In 2000, LG launched an internet-ready refrigerator (Figure 18). Complete with a 15-inch LCD screen, Ethernet port and television tuner, the device allowed users to leave messages, monitor contents without opening the door, keep calendars, and download recipe and nutritional information.

Figure 18   Just some of LG's internet-ready appliances: (top) a microwave oven; (bottom) the internet refrigerator, a washing machine and a tumble drier

At US$8000, the refrigerator sold in extremely limited numbers in both South Korea and the USA.

Other manufacturers have incorporated internet connectivity into household devices such as microwave ovens, washing machines and coffee makers, where it could be used to deliver information such as recipes or how to get better washing performance, or have the machine inform a service centre when it needs maintenance. Perhaps surprisingly, none of them have been very successful.

Activity 27 (exploratory)

Suggest a few reasons for the lack of success of these internet-enabled smart devices.

Comment

You probably didn't have to work too hard on this. Here are some possibilities:

1   These devices are much more expensive than a conventional product. Customers could buy an ordinary appliance and several laptops for the same price.

2   Users generally use relatively few of the settings on conventional devices – they would hardly see a need for yet more.

3   Customers don't want to be lumbered with a cumbersome and potentially obsolete product.

4   The internet is much more accessible using small, convenient and portable devices such as mobile phones and laptops.

Despite these setbacks, LG has continued to push ahead, investing heavily in LG HomNet, a self-configuring network that connects household appliances by wireless links or over mains electrical cables using LG's Living Network Control Protocol (LnCP). Devices can be controlled from a PC, or even remotely through a mobile phone. Again, however, the technology has not yet been commercially successful.

PC bangs and video games

South Korea may have delivered on the promise of fast internet connections to every home, but the most vibrant part of South Korea's online culture is found in tens of thousands of *PC bangs*. These cyber cafés offer high-speed internet access, comfortable seating and food and drink. The high-density housing that has made universal broadband possible in South Korea brings its own problems for young people – in particular, lack of space to entertain friends or even set up a computer. For Korean children and young adults, PC bangs are as much a social space as a place where they can go online.

The success of the PC bang owes much to video games, and to one game in particular: *StarCraft*. This US science fiction strategy game, although released in 1998, remains phenomenally popular in South Korea. Of the 9.5 million copies sold, nearly half were bought in South Korea.

When *StarCraft* was released, domestic broadband was rare in South Korea, but it was already available through PC bangs, which were thus able to offer high-speed networked gaming. Soon *StarCraft* had become an inextricable part of the PC bang culture: PC bangs ran competitions across their internal networks, which soon expanded to pit one PC bang against another. Eventually, the Korea Pro Gaming League was established – a nationwide association of professional video game players whose live matches draw crowds of up 100 000 people and are followed by millions on cable television (Figure 19).

Figure 19   A *StarCraft* match televised by MBCGame

PC bangs and *StarCraft* provided inspiration for the South Korean video game industry, which has grown by 25 per cent year on year and now has annual revenues exceeding US$4 billion. Near-universal broadband access has directly influenced the types of games developed by South Korean studios, which have specialised in developing MMORPGs that are utterly dependent on high-speed networks.

South Korean studios make about half their income from domestic customers, but foreign sales are rapidly increasing as overseas players begin to experience similar broadband access to South Korea. At the forefront of this new export success is *MapleStory*, which boasts over 20 million users in its native South Korea and a further 10 million across the rest of the world – between them spending US$200 million on the game in 2010 alone.

Future cities

If there is one symbol of South Korea's rush to the future it is Songdo (Figure 20), a city covering six square kilometres that is rising from reclaimed land near Incheon, west of Seoul. Begun in 2006 as a collaboration between government and private business, the project will eventually cost more than US$40 billion, house some 65 000 people and employ more than 300 000 workers. When completed, Songdo will have an airport linked to the city by a 7 km bridge, a world-class convention centre and two of the tallest buildings in Asia. Its developers hope that the city's superb infrastructure will make it the most attractive place to do business in Asia.

Figure 20   The skyline of Songdo under construction in mid-2009

Songdo has been specifically designed as a place where companies and researchers can explore the usability of new ubiquitous technologies on the scale of a whole city. In laboratories, the environment is carefully controlled; in Songdo, the bustle of a busy city will demonstrate how devices cope with unplanned events, crowds, congestion or disasters.

A city-wide telecommunications backbone is being built by Cisco Systems as a demonstration of their Smart+Connected Communities initiative. Not only will factories, offices and homes be wired, but network access will be truly ubiquitous. Even the streets and walls of Songdo will have network access points, and the city will be bathed in wireless networks. Most cities have a mishmash of incompatible networks; Songdo will have a single network controlling everything, from the very large (e.g. regulating the city's energy consumption) to the very small (e.g. controlling systems in a single apartment). Developers promise that ubicomp technology will reduce Songdo's environmental impact through better energy, water and waste management systems, and by monitoring traffic flows and public transport usage. Songdo is an example of what has become known as a technology city (see Box 5).

> ### Box 5 Technology cities
>
> More than half a trillion US dollars is currently being spent on building technology cities around the world, none of which are in established industrial nations. Technology cities are places where new technologies can be researched and demonstrated. Many of them house universities and research laboratories, and some offer tax incentives for foreign investors to locate operations inside the city.
>
> Saudi Arabia alone is home to four technology cities, which when complete will have a combined population of 2.5 million people. Nearby Qatar has two. India is building Gujarat International Finance Tec-City (GIFT), whilst China is constructing a new technology city of its own at Meixi Lake.

Activity 28 (exploratory)

Songdo's developers have created a number of videos demonstrating how new technology will be used in the city, one of which is supplied in the resources page associated with this part. This will give you a good overview of the connections and services that will make Songdo into a technology city.

Songdo will host the Chadwick International School, an offshoot of a private Californian school where all tuition is in English. The campus features lavish theatres, libraries and laboratories as well as bright classrooms, but it is its use of technology that is eye-opening. Classroom 2.0, as it has inevitably been called, is a form of synchronous distance education somewhat like Open University online tutorials (but rather more expensive!). The school's classrooms are linked by two Cisco telepresence suites to the parent campus in California, allowing students on both campuses to join virtual classes, and staff on one campus to lecture students on the other.

Activity 29 (exploratory)

In the resources page associated with this part on the TU100 website, you will find a video that provides an introduction to the Songdo International School. When convenient, watch this video and make notes on how broadband and telepresence technologies can be used for educational purposes.

4.3 Estonia

Estonia is home to a number of high-tech computing, biotechnology and engineering companies. Perhaps the most famous Estonian product is Skype – software that enables telephone conversation over the internet. However, Estonia's most interesting use of its digital communications is in the field of electronic government.

You were introduced to Skype in Block 4 Part 3.

Identity cards

Government promotion of electronic services is tied to Estonia's national identity card. Most European countries require adult citizens to carry such a card. Traditionally these have taken the form of either plastic cards or small books similar to passports, usually including a photograph. Estonia's government was one of the first to replace paper identity documents with a credit-card-sized photo smart card (Figure 21), which not only allows Estonians to access government services but also acts as a travel document within the Schengen Area of the European Union.

The Schengen Area comprises 25 European countries that have agreed to allow citizens to pass between member states without showing a passport. The UK is not a member of the system.

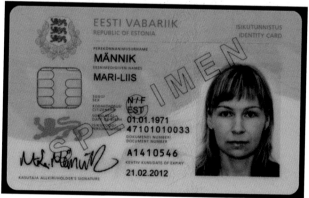

Figure 21   **The front face of the Estonian national identity card issued to citizens**

Embedded in the card is a microchip (the shiny gold rectangle towards the left-hand side of the card in the figure), which is similar to those found in modern UK passports. This holds the cardholder's name, ID number, sex, citizenship or residency permit, card number and expiry date in an unprotected file, along with two *digital certificates* allowing the cardholder to access various services:

You learned about digital certificates in Block 5 Part 3.

1   the authentication certificate – used to confirm that the card is genuine and being used by the actual holder

2   the signing certificate – used to authenticate or encrypt documents being sent via email or the Web (Figure 22).

Both certificates also contain the individual's email address. In addition, the card contains a pair of private keys – one for each certificate – that authenticate the card itself and can only be used when the user enters the PIN for that key. The card slots into a dedicated card reader terminal or a card reader connected to a PC by USB, and users can then authenticate transactions using their PIN.

Digiallkirjastatud dokument sinu arvutis

Digiallkirjastatud dokumenti võib aga samaaegselt lausa miljonis eri kohas hoida.

Figure 22   A still from a promotional video for the Estonian ID card explaining how it can be used to authenticate electronic documents

Estonian identity cards contain little private data that cannot be found elsewhere, and so not much has been done to protect the contents of the card. However, the more personal data associated with the data on the card can only be viewed by the individual or by officials at a government office.

Since adopting the national ID card, Estonia has pioneered other forms of digital identification, all tied to the master identity database. Digi-ID is a limited form of identification that can only be used for online services, whilst Mobiil-ID uses special SIM cards in mobile phones to authenticate online banking transactions and digital signatures.

Email for everyone

Every adult Estonian citizen and resident has a government-issued 'eesti.ee' email address, intended to last for a person's lifetime and acting as the point of contact between government and citizens. The government does not act as an email service provider, so an online form is used to redirect mail from a citizen's government address to their personal email account. If a citizen does not have a personal email account then their messages are simply discarded. All eesti.ee addresses are publicly available, but there is strict legislation forbidding the sending of spam and abusive email to the accounts.

Electronic elections

> You trust your money with the internet, and you won't trust your vote? I don't think so.
>
> Tarvi Martens, project manager for Estonia's 2007 e-voting project
> (quoted in Borland, 2007)

The first trials of electronic voting were conducted in Australia in 2001. In the same year, Estonia's government proposed that e-voting should be introduced as an alternative to paper ballots. In doing so, it was making a confident statement about the importance of information technology to the country's future, and its ambition to be among the most advanced Western countries.

Traditionally, voting in elections has been paper-based. Voters are given a ballot paper; they mark one or more candidates and place their ballot in a sealed box. The ballot papers are then counted manually. This process can be lengthy and is error-prone. Superficially, e-voting is an attractive alternative: there is no paper involved, people can vote from home, work or abroad, and the results can be known almost immediately. The necessary software and hardware already exist. Yet very few fully electronic elections have been conducted. Why?

The question bedevilling e-voting systems is simply this: 'who is actually casting the vote?' Any secure voting system must ensure two things:

1   only registered voters can cast a vote

2   the person casting the vote is who they say they are.

Election law in Estonia requires that anyone who wishes to vote must present an Estonian national identity card at the polling station. Internet votes are authenticated by the authentication certificate on a voter's identity card, and are cast using a standard web browser. E-voting takes place over several days leading up to the actual election; rather surprisingly, e-voters are allowed to change their vote as many times as they like until the polls close, simply by casting a new e-vote – which invalidates earlier ones.

During the count, each encrypted voting form is first checked to ensure that it has not been corrupted in transit and does not duplicate a paper vote. For all valid votes, the information linking the e-vote to the individual who cast it is removed and their vote recorded. Finally, the e-vote totals are added to those for paper votes and the result announced.

Activity 30 (self-assessment)

On voting day, Mikk casts an electronic vote for Hele and then goes to work. During his lunch break he decides he would prefer to vote for Eliisabet. He casts another electronic vote. Has Mikk voted for two people?

In 2005, Estonia tested its e-voting technology in municipal elections across the country; less than 2% of registered voters (just 9317 people) chose to vote electronically. Yet amongst the mountain of statistics generated by these elections was one encouraging fact. Of all e-voters, 61% had used their identity cards for the first time to authenticate their vote. It was hoped that once people had used their cards to access one government service, they would be willing to do so again in the future.

> The goal is to make things easier for people, to increase participation. No one has managed to prove that e-voting actually raises participation, so that remains unanswered. But this gives people another possibility.

Arne Koitmäe, National Electoral Commission (quoted in Borland, 2007)

Estonia's next nationwide elections were held in February 2007. This time, 30 275 e-votes were cast – approximately 3.5% of the electorate. The demographics of the e-voters in the 2007 elections are revealed in the chart in Figure 23.

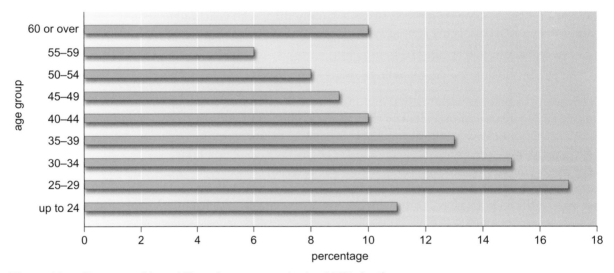

Figure 23   Demographics of Estonian e-voters in the 2007 elections

Activity 31 (exploratory)

Does the chart show any significant differences between the age groups?

Comment

Perhaps predictably, e-voting was most popular amongst voters aged 25–39. It was least popular amongst people aged 55–59, although – perhaps surprisingly – popular amongst the eldest voters.

A gradual acceptance of e-voting by the Estonian electorate was suggested two years later, when the 2009 municipal elections saw 104 415 people (9.5% of the electorate) cast e-votes.

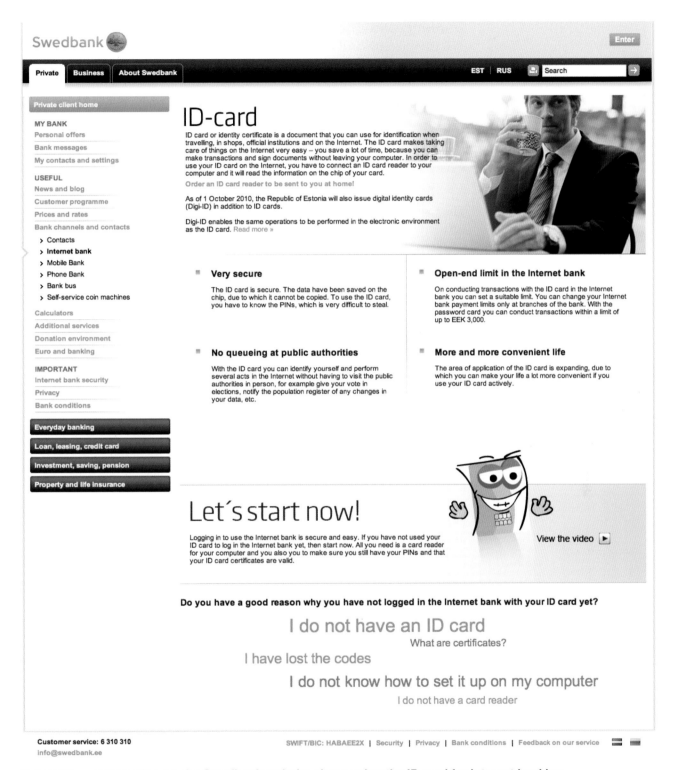

Figure 24   Information on the Swedbank website about using the ID card for internet banking

Banking and shopping

The Estonian ID card has become a genuinely popular technology, partly because it is useful for non-government services – especially internet banking – where the card adds an extra level of fraud protection. For instance, Swedbank – one of the largest banks in Estonia – encourages customers to use their national ID cards as authentication for its online services (Figure 24). Increasingly, the ID card has also been required in other businesses where significant amounts of money or personal information are exchanged.

The Swedbank page encourages users to switch to internet banking secured by their identity cards. As you might expect, there is a strong emphasis on the convenience and ease of use of the cards as well as the greater levels of security they offer for online transactions. A great deal of time and effort has been given over to reassuring users that the cards will make their lives easier and are nothing to be afraid of. Text and video is used to explain that whilst customers might begin using their cards for online banking, the same card will give them easy access to many other government and commercial services. Finally, Swedbank customers can order one of the all-important card readers that will let them begin using the service.

Swedbank's site is provided not only in Estonian and Russian for residents, but also in English to target the large number of foreign employees of multinational companies attracted to Estonia.

Since 2003, the ID card has been used as a virtual ticket (Figure 25) in the cities of Tallinn and Tartu. Under the Pilet scheme, holders of Estonian ID cards can set up online accounts, linked to their personal ID number and accessed through the card, in which they deposit money for purchasing tickets for public transport and events (Figure 26).

Figure 25   Another still from a promotional video for the Estonian ID card, this time demonstrating how it can be used as a virtual ticket

Figure 26   Website allowing users of the Pilet service to buy tickets for a swimming pool

4.4 Bangladesh

As you learned in Session 2, Bangladesh has extremely poor communications, so the hi-tech options for economic and social development open to Estonia and South Korea are simply not available to it. Nevertheless, even here, mobile technology is making an impact.

CellBazaar

Buying and selling online turned eBay into one of the most successful of the early dotcom companies. In Bangladesh, CellBazaar (Figure 27) allows millions of people to do the same, simply by using an SMS-equipped mobile phone (i.e. a mobile phone capable of sending and receiving text messages). Founded by Kamel S. Quadir, a Bangladeshi MIT graduate, CellBazaar operates solely inside Bangladesh in partnership with Grameen Telecom.

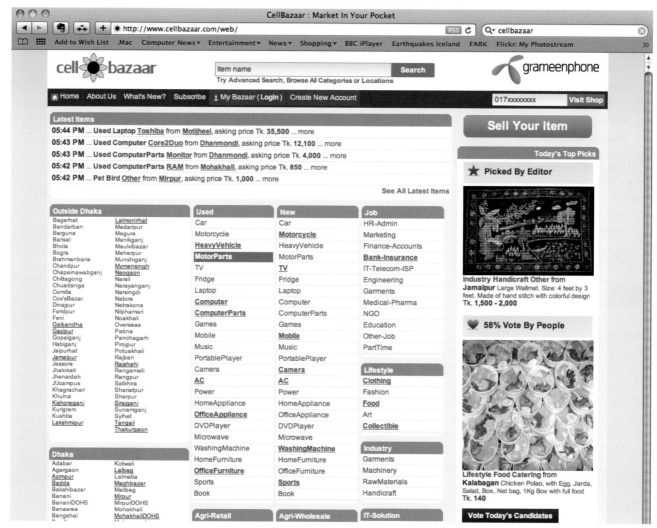

Figure 27   The CellBazaar front page in early 2011

CellBazaar has had to confront two problems that prevent Bangladeshi citizens from using a site such as eBay:

1 *Lack of computers.* Relatively few Bangladeshis own or have access to a networked computer; whilst smart phones do have the necessary browsers, they constitute only a tiny share of the Bangladeshi market. The less sophisticated phones that dominate the market lack web browsers.

2 *Lack of credit cards.* Most Bangladeshis have no access to credit or debit cards, so conventional online payments cannot be processed.

CellBazaar has been able to tackle the first issue, but not the second. Most of CellBazaar's functions are available through an SMS-enabled mobile phone; clients browse listings by sending and responding to SMS messages.

Whilst eBay users can use the site's payment facilities to buy items, CellBazaar only provides the buyer with the seller's mobile phone number. Besides the low availability of credit cards, there are also cultural reasons for this:

1 Many transactions will be local, since personal and public transport are not widely available and postal charges are high.

2 Most sales will have a suggested price that is open to haggling, rather than a fixed price.

During 2009 alone, the number of people using CellBazaar grew from 1.5 million to 4 million. Users range from urban professionals looking for jobs and rented accommodation to farmers in remote villages who, using village phones, are seeking up-to-date market information for their produce.

Cyclone warnings

Most of Bangladesh lies less than 10 metres above sea level, and so is highly vulnerable to flooding – both from the Ganges and Brahmaputra rivers, and from tropical cyclones that form yearly in the Bay of Bengal. These storms gather power over the ocean, gradually moving north until they hit land, bringing torrential rain, high winds and 'storm surges' – huge mounds of water pushed up from the ocean's surface by the wind, which can breach river banks and cause catastrophic flooding. The death toll from the 1970 Cyclone Bhola was over 500 000. Twenty-one years later, Cyclone 02B devastated the Chittagong region with 255 kmph winds and a 6 metre storm surge, killing 138 000 people and leaving more than 10 million homeless. Even when a cyclone does not result in loss of human life, it will wipe out livestock, pollute the ground with sewage and sea water, and cause enormous damage; for instance, 2007's Cyclone Sidr (Figure 28) caused damage of more than US$1.7 billion.

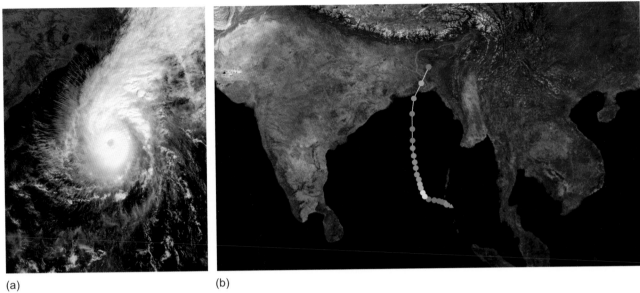

(a)　　　　　　　　　　　　　　　　　　(b)

Figure 28　**(a) Cyclone Sidr approaches the coast of Bangladesh – the patch at the centre is known as the 'eye'; (b) the path of Cyclone Sidr from its origin in the Indian Ocean to its eventual dissipation over Assam (the orange and red dots show the maximum intensity of the storm)**

Activity 32 (self-assessment)

Flood warning systems on the Ganges and Brahmaputra rivers are poorly implemented and many thousands of people continue to die unnecessarily. In the resources page associated with this part you will find a link to a paper discussing the design and introduction of an automated flood monitoring system in another part of the world, Honduras in Central America, written by researchers at MIT. Read Sections V to VII and answer the following questions.

(a) Give two reasons why volunteer-based human warning systems may not work.

(b) Identify the key components in the automated system and the technologies used.

(c) What recurring costs must be avoided and why?

(d) Briefly list some of the non-technological problems experienced in the project.

(e) Why is the involvement of the community and the government essential?

(f) From the information given in the paper, would you say that this is a form of ubiquitous computing?

Satellite tracking of storms, allowing predictions of their severity and the time, date and precise site of landfall (Figure 29), has been possible for many years. Bangladeshi officials can access data from satellites operated by NASA and NOAA (the US National Oceanic and Atmospheric Administration), but the country still faces a real challenge in warning its people of approaching disaster. Following the devastating 1991 cyclone, a Comprehensive Cyclone Preparedness Programme (CCPP) – jointly planned, operated and managed by the Ministry of Disaster Management and Relief and the Bangladesh Red Crescent Society – was put in place. This provided coastal areas with an early warning system: up to 42 000 volunteers use bicycles and megaphones to warn residents of imminent flooding. But warnings that work well in the West – television and radio weather forecasts, telephone alerts, etc. – are useless in remote areas of Bangladesh, where such technologies are unavailable.

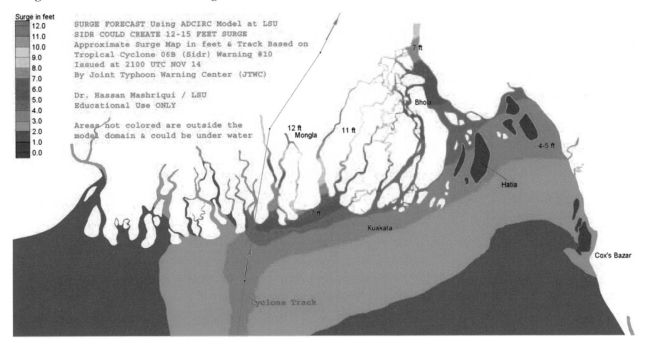

Figure 29   A supercomputer prediction of the storm surge generated by Cyclone Sidr in 2007: the colours show the height of the surge, with red, orange and yellow being the highest levels (up to 4 metres)

Mobile phone ownership in Bangladesh has risen during the last few years (although as a percentage of the population it remains low). Much of the country now has some level of mobile access, and services are almost universal in populous areas on the most fertile land – those places most likely to be flooded. Emergency messages could be broadcast to a population, allowing them to make preparations or to leave the area. In 2005, a paper discussing such a role for mobile phone technologies was presented to a conference on government. At this time, although only 6% of the Bangladeshi population had direct access to mobile phones, some were available in almost all communities – even if an individual did not have a phone, they probably knew someone who did. And by 2008, more than a quarter of Bangladeshis owned a mobile phone.

Grameenphone is Bangladesh's largest mobile phone operator. It is a joint venture between Grameen Telecom and the Norwegian telecoms company Telenor.

In 2009, two of Bangladesh's largest mobile phone operators, Grameenphone and Teletalk, piloted automated warning messages for subscribers living in two especially vulnerable areas, Sirajganj and Cox's Bazar. The system uses SMS to deliver simple text warnings – but unlike normal messages, the entire warning is always placed on the phone's screen rather than being diverted to a mailbox or only showing the sender's name.

Activity 33 (exploratory)

Do you think SMS is the most appropriate technology for delivering this information? Would some other system be more informative or more easily understood?

Comment

MMS stands for Multimedia Messaging Service – a way of sending messages to and from mobile phones that incorporate still pictures, video or sound. Unlike SMS, there is no single standard for MMS, which leads to incompatibilities between handsets and operators.

SMS is the simplest method of delivering information, and is supported by almost all mobile phones. More sophisticated delivery mechanisms such as MMS or web pages only work through more sophisticated handsets, which may be too expensive for most users.

It is certainly possible to use a mobile phone without being able to read (although it is unlikely that an illiterate person could afford one). It is questionable whether SMS messages would be meaningful to those with very low levels of literacy. Possibly pre-recorded or computer-generated spoken messages might be more useful, as they could offer detailed information. Using data about the phone's location, directions to the nearest shelter could be given. However, such a system would need considerable investment.

4.5 Conclusion

This session has given you some indication of the uses to which the wide range of developments in ICT around the world have been put. Clearly the development status of a particular country has an impact on the type of projects that emerge. Some of these differences can be explained by the available infrastructure, whilst others are attempts to accommodate the expectations of their citizens.

South Korea is perhaps the most extreme example of the adoption of technology; the country's economy is being reshaped not only to deliver high-technology goods and services, but to export them to the rest of the world.

By contrast, poorer countries such as Kenya yield exemplars of appropriate technology, where the benefits of ICTs are being delivered in a manner that does not place undue stresses on fragile and frequently under-resourced societies. Many examples in this context show how individuals and small communities can benefit from greater access to information – whether on health, the law or even market prices – and from a reduction in the costs of goods and services (cheaper bank transfers or access to clean, reliable water). Many economists would hold that as individuals become richer, it is inevitable that the economy as a whole will grow as these people consume more goods and services, although real life is rarely so simple.

This session should have helped you with the following learning outcomes.

- Describe the concept of a digital divide and some of its different aspects.
- Describe the different scales of the digital divide (local, national and global).
- Describe approaches to technological development in a number of different countries and explain the reasons for these approaches.
- Analyse examples of appropriate technology in the context of the digital divide.
- Use appropriate statistical techniques to analyse aspects of various digital divides.

5 Nepal – a case study in connection

This session (including Activities 34 and 35) is delivered online. It can be found in the resources page associated with this part on the TU100 website.

Closing the digital divide

6

I ended Session 1 of this part with four challenging questions. I asked whether closing the digital divide would:

- be possible?
- be desirable?
- cure poverty?
- really matter?

Let's now return to these questions. It must already be obvious that the issues are very complex – a web of political, demographic, ethnic, cultural, educational, historical and geographical factors. Nor is there just one kind of digital divide – there are many. Nevertheless, we should at least attempt some tentative answers.

6.1 Is it possible?

Looking back at the experiences of African nations, Bangladesh and Nepal, we can see that two of the main barriers to closing the digital divide between them and the developed world appear to be the massive amount of funding needed to establish and maintain the required technological infrastructure of communications networks; and the fact that even when the infrastructure exists, it may not be affordable to a large number of people.

Infrastructure costs

Perhaps the most obvious point is that technological development, particularly building and sustaining the required infrastructure, requires enormous infusions of money over long periods. In South Korea this came from government borrowing and from well-established banks. In Estonia it came largely from foreign investment from neighbouring countries. Poorer nations have limited access to such funds.

However, as you have seen with the examples of Bangladesh and Kenya, money can be raised in a variety of ways: by new banks (Grameen's Village Phone), through foreign aid (M-PESA) and by private companies (M-PESA).

Communications costs

The experience of Bangladesh seemed to show that the cost of accessing information, especially through mobile phones, has generally fallen steeply. But in reality, as a proportion of income, communications are still expensive in the developing world. In 2008, ResearchICTAfrica published *Towards Evidence-based ICT Policy and Regulation: ICT access and usage in Africa*, which surveyed the cost of communications across the continent. Figure 30 shows the results for five countries including South Africa and Kenya.

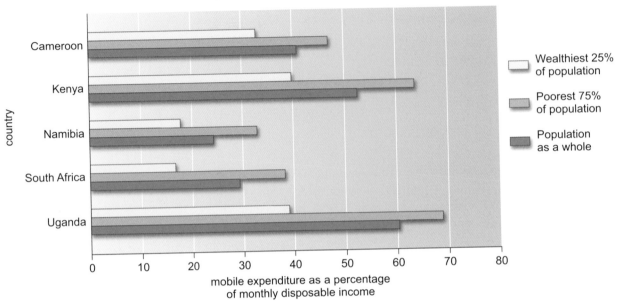

Figure 30   **The cost of communications in five African countries (data taken from Gillwald and Stork, 2008, p. 15)**

These examples are typical: in many African countries people spend a significant percentage of their income on mobile communications – often more than half of their total disposable income (the money left over after tax). Few people in the UK will spend more than 5% of their disposable income on mobile communications; in Kenya the average is 52.5%.

Possible reasons for this difference include the following:

1   Mobile communications are disproportionately expensive in Kenya.

2   Kenyans are choosing to spend money on mobile communications.

3   Kenyans are forced to spend money on mobile communications.

The third possibility is especially disturbing, and there is some evidence to suggest that it might actually be happening. In a country with few fixed lines, SMS is essential to finding casual work. Even if a worker has no other need for a mobile phone, they need one to find employment. And since most unskilled casual work is poorly paid, mobile costs account for a high proportion of that worker's income.

There are other cases where access to a mobile phone has become absolutely necessary. Recall that Kenya's LIFELINK solar pumps only accept wireless payments from M-PESA accounts. Superficially the pump is an attractive idea, but again it requires people to own a mobile phone whether they want one or not. Furthermore, the payment system is restricted to Safaricom users. A user cannot switch to any other telecom provider.

Catching up or falling behind?

One theory of economic development proposes that countries starting at a relative disadvantage to more developed nations will grow more quickly. Countries pioneering new technologies make mistakes or fail to exploit their potential quickly, whereas those following on later can avoid such pitfalls. For instance, it took the UK more than a century to industrialise; today, China, Brazil and India are doing it in a single generation.

So, does 'catching up' help to bridge the digital divide? Figure 31 suggests that in some cases it might.

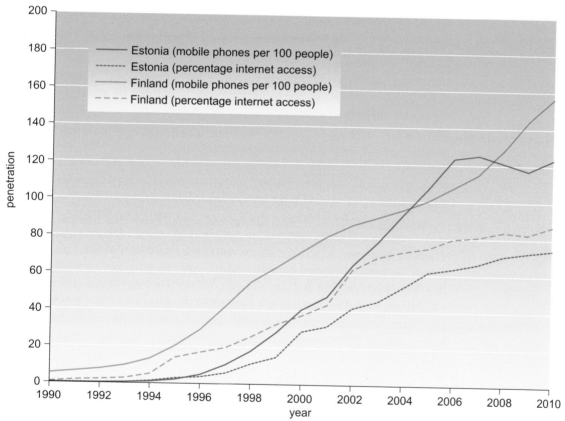

Figure 31 **Relative rates of penetration of mobile phones and internet access in Finland and Estonia**

Activity 36 (exploratory)

How do you think the graph in Figure 31 supports the 'catching up' theory of economic development? Can you think of a reason why the growth in the number of mobile phone subscriptions in Estonia reverses sharply from 2007 to 2009?

Comment

The graph plots the adoption of mobile phones (solid lines) and internet access (dashes) in Estonia and Finland between 1990 and 2008. Wealthy Finland experiences continuous growth. Estonia begins at a lower level, but adoption increases rapidly until Estonians own more phones per capita than Finns. According to the 'catching up' model, Finland's early experiments with a novel technology benefitted Estonia's industry, which targeted customers with products that had already proven to be popular.

The decline in Estonian mobile phone subscriptions occurred during a sharp economic downtown that began in 2007 in the financial sectors in a number of new economies around Europe. With a large financial sector, Estonia was hit especially hard; its economy contracted by 14% in 2009 alone and unemployment rose sharply. As businesses failed and household incomes were put under pressure, people cancelled some of their mobile phone contracts.

Internet adoption is a different story. Here, both countries pioneered the technology at the same time, and growth rates were roughly the same. Differences between the countries might be explained by the comparative wealth of individual citizens. It is interesting that the economic trouble of 2007 onwards did not see a fall in internet users. More research would be needed to find an explanation; it is possible that internet users are generally more wealthy and better insulated from any economic problems, or people might consider internet access an essential part of modern life and be unwilling to part with it even in difficult times.

There is, however, a perhaps more worrying limitation of the 'catching up' theory. A less developed country might well catch up with a more developed nation, but the developed country does not stand still in the meantime; it will be developing new technologies of its own. And since wealthier countries have greater resources – not only of money, but of skilled labour – the digital divide between richer and poorer may actually widen rather than narrow.

6.2   Is it desirable?

The computer on your desk and the mobile phone in your pocket are Western (often North American) technologies, and they include many aspects of the culture that created them – for instance, their cases are designed to coordinate with Western homes and offices. Computer software uses concepts such as 'folders' and 'trash cans' (or the more environmentally friendly 'recycle bins'), which may not be familiar outside the West.

Perhaps the most significant cultural aspect of computing is the use of the English language. Despite attempts by software manufacturers to 'localise' software by translating terms into other languages, some measure of proficiency in English is vital in order to use a computer effectively. Even as new a technology as the *World Wide* Web has only recently become accessible to large parts of the world: it was only in 2009 that it became possible to write URLs using Chinese and Japanese ideograms, with the first international domains being created the following year. In addition, many computer programs still only support languages that are written horizontally from the top left of the page, despite the alternative styles of Hebrew, Arabic, Mandarin and Japanese. Above all, there is an enormous dearth of software translated into local languages, either because of a perceived lack of demand or because there are simply not enough skilled translators.

As a result of all this, the transfer of technologies from the West to the developing world carries with it a large number of specific conventions (of language, of usage and of purpose) that new users of those technologies are forced to adopt – even if the conventions in question are not compatible with their own cultures. For this reason, some commentators have argued that (often well-meaning) attempts to close the digital divide are just another form of *cultural imperialism*.

> Perhaps the biggest mistake we have made as technology [pioneers] is assuming that everyone should adopt our own particular flavor of technology.
>
> Despite their merits, our need for speed and information obsession in the US and most of the West is not universally accepted. In other places there is a greater emphasis on downtime and not uptime. In many parts of the world connectedness still has more to do with direct family and community interactions than with iPhones, wireless laptops and online social networking.

Lamb, 2007

Do you agree with this sentiment? Or do you feel that this is just another piece of Western liberal condescension towards the developing world?

Cultural imperialism is the practice of imposing the culture of one society onto another to the detriment of local customs, knowledge and values.

6.3 Can it cure poverty?

This is the biggest question of all. Can living standards in the developing world really be raised to those of developed countries by modern information and computer technologies?

One of the greatest causes of poverty is lack of access to basic education. Children and adults are denied access to education by many factors, including:

* the inability of a country to afford universal, free education, or only being able to offer it for very young people

- a lack of suitable schools, teaching materials and teachers
- inadequate transport systems that cannot deliver children to schools
- cultural factors that deny education to parts of the population, especially to women
- an economic requirement for people to work rather than remain in education.

The question is whether some, or all, or any of these problems have *technological* solutions.

One Laptop Per Child

Can the computer eliminate poverty? Professor Nicholas Negroponte of the One Laptop Per Child initiative, discussed in Session 4, certainly thinks so. However, even such a generous and well-intentioned project as OLPC has attracted much criticism.

Activity 37 (exploratory)

Using a range of online resources, create a bullet list of criticisms of OLPC. Don't forget to record your sources for future reference.

Comment

Some of the criticisms levelled at OLPC include the following.

- *Cost* – in an impoverished country, a price of US$100 represents as much of an outlay as US$1000 in a more developed country. Unless the machine is donated, it might be unaffordable. In some cases XO-1s have been resold by their users, who can find more immediate uses for the money.
- *Scale* – it is simply economically impossible to provide a laptop to every child in very large countries such as India and China.
- *Training* – even a computer designed for children requires some trained users to help others. OLPC has been criticised for not providing assistance to teachers who would then be able to instruct the users.
- *Infrastructure* – computers don't exist in isolation. They require maintenance or replacements. In addition, computers are often most useful when used with other technologies such as printers and cameras, all of which have their own costs.
- *Connectivity* – in the countries targeted by OLPC, internet access is generally slow, intermittent or unavailable, which not only restricts the user's ability to access information but also prevents them from obtaining the large number of applications designed for the computer.

Negroponte had aimed to sell 15 million laptops by the end of 2008; however, in May 2009 only about one million had been sold. Subscribers to OLPC's high-profile 'Give one, get one' scheme – in which consumers could buy their own XO-1 and donate a second – fell from 83 500 in 2007 to 12 500 the following year. The decline was put down to poor coordination of the 2007 scheme and failures by OLPC's partners to ship machines in a timely fashion. As a result, in 2009, OLPC was forced to make 50% of its staff redundant, reduce the salaries of its remaining staff and restructure its operations (Musil, 2009).

Supporters of OLPC argue that the XO-1 has proved the demand for such a machine; not only have more than a million machines been produced, but competing machines have been designed – and not just for the developing world. Competitors took the ideas behind the XO-1 beyond their original context, developing them into the netbook computer.

However, OLPC's detractors make powerful arguments of their own. According to Knut Foseide, President of FAIR (Fair Allocation of Infotech Resources):

> Every year in the west we destroy tens of millions of PCs which are far better than OLPC and which would cost not much more than a tenth of OLPC to put to use in developing countries. This is established technology which can run the latest software and get the recipients up to western levels of IT technology without delays. In the present circumstances this is a far better alternative. For western organisations such as MIT, OLPC and their sub-contractors to benefit by transferring expensive and risky technology to the world's poorest countries, without any documented need for it, looks like exploitation to those of us who are really committed to global aid work.

FAIR, 2007

According to Jon Evans (2009), writing in *The Walrus* magazine, there are two basic reasons why the OLPC project has been a failure:

1 Technological problems – the XO-1 is slow, its screen and keyboard are too small, and it suffers from connectivity problems. In short, 'the XO laptop is a piece of crap'.

2 'It was a bad idea to begin with' because ICTs had already penetrated developing countries in the form of mobile phones. In Evans' view, what Negroponte and his partners should have come up with was 'One *Smartphone* Per Child'.

Many critics would claim that the idea of solving the desperate problems of some developing nations just by dumping computers in poor communities is simply naïve – stemming from a blinkered Western belief that technology solves all problems. It is generally accepted that poverty rarely has a single cause. It is the consequence of many complex, interlocking problems, and so can have no single solution. We might accept that technology could solve *some* issues of poverty, but many other issues must be addressed first.

Priorities

It would be hard to argue that access to technology is more important than primary healthcare, universal education and basic sanitation. If a child dies before reaching maturity, education ceases to matter. In poor countries, the benefits of spending government money on improving the fundamentals of life must surely outweigh those of high technologies. As Marthe Dansokho, a delegate from Cameroon speaking at the World Summit on the Information Society in Tunis in December 2005, pointed out:

> African women who do most of the work in the countryside don't have time to sit with their children and research what crops they should be planting. We know our land and wisdom is passed down through the generations. What is needed is clean water and real schools.

Quoted in Smith, 2005

A counter-argument might be that technology is already transforming lives in very poor societies – as in Bangladesh and East Africa. Here, appropriate technology is being introduced by private organisations, often in association with aid agencies. Rather than the government directing development, individuals and small groups of people are finding their own way.

6.4 Does it really matter?

It has been argued that lack of access to ICTs will leave a developing country's citizens too poorly educated to compete in the global economy. The assumption here is that education is *only* about achieving economic objectives. But a broader view of education might look beyond mere economic success to issues such as meeting local needs, enhancing social justice and human rights, and ensuring cultural and political freedom. For this reason, discussion of the global digital divide cannot be separated from questions of values and how ICTs can be best used to benefit societies – not only through wealth generation, but also by allowing people to express themselves through politics, literature, music and so on.

When deciding on ICT needs, it is important to consider the difference between real needs of users and artificial needs generated by others. Many of the technologies used in the developing world are imported from the

West, and as you have learned, they come with certain cultural assumptions. They may also come with sophisticated marketing designed to increase revenue for the supplier.

> When computer companies such as AOL or other internet providers avow that they would like to abolish the [digital] divide, this is [...] just sound business practice. Saying that everyone should be on-line (that everyone *needs* to be on-line) will presumably generate more customers.
>
> Moss, 2002, p. 164

You've learned that a number of successful projects address basic problems by deploying *appropriate technology*. Many of these involve a combination of different stakeholders – the public sector (national governments), the private sector (companies and multinationals), non-governmental organisations, advocacy groups, think tanks and representation from the target audience. Different stakeholders are likely to have different demands from, and degrees of influence on, a project. The success, or otherwise, of a project will depend on whether these issues can be resolved to the satisfaction of all parties.

This is a computing and technology module, but perhaps we can finish with a rather unexpected thought: ***one can live perfectly happily without access to computers and communications technologies***. Throughout history, throughout the world, people have chosen to retreat from the march of technology. Some have done so for religious reasons and some as a personal protest against the path that civilisation has chosen to take. Box 6 describes one such community.

Box 6 A different approach to technology: the Amish

Perhaps the most well-known group who appear to live in a non-technological society are the Amish Mennonites, some quarter of a million people living in the eastern USA and Canada. The Amish are the descendants of Swiss and German settlers who fled persecution in Europe so that they could continue to practise their pacifist beliefs. Amish teachings hold that life should remain simple and should never be easy, that sloth and vanity are profound sins, and that tightly knit communities flourish and should not be unnecessarily dependent on outside society. One consequence of these beliefs has been that Amish society has become increasingly distinct from wider US society, and it is in the Amish attitude to technology that this is perhaps most apparent.

The Amish do not believe technology is inherently evil, but they do believe it has the potential to undermine parts of their belief system. Certain technologies are essentially forbidden by the

Amish. Cars would allow people to live further apart and weaken family and community ties, whilst mains electricity would make the Amish dependent on an outside utility, and the technologies made possible by electricity – such as televisions and radios – might make people lazy.

Beyond these core technologies, there is a surprising diversity of opinion towards the adoption of technology. What is forbidden in one Amish community may be permissible in another, since acceptance or rejection is generally addressed by local churches and bishops at six-month intervals. Religious leaders receive petitions from their congregations and, in consultation with the community, attempt to reconcile the genuine benefits of certain technologies with the demands of their faith. Thus the Amish have adopted some technologies when it can be demonstrated that they bring real benefits to communities and do not conflict with Amish beliefs.

So whilst mains electricity is not acceptable to the Amish, batteries and solar power – which are independent of external suppliers – are permitted to power devices such as calculators and computers (although not networked devices), as well as even simpler technologies such as reading lights for the elderly or partially sighted. Even telephones, the most connected of all devices, are found in most Amish communities. However, they are almost never found in the home, but are relegated to booths located on the edges of villages. This allows the Amish to take advantage of the telephone whilst avoiding its unwanted intrusion into the privacy of their homes.

The Amish are often held up as an anachronism hostile to technological progress, but in reality they have developed an extremely sophisticated relationship with technology that is perhaps much more thought through than the attitude taken by those of us who have embraced modern technologies and are now grappling with the consequences.

It is obvious that no one should ever be compelled to use digital technologies if they conflict with deeply held personal beliefs. But the *option* to use them should be available to all.

Activity 38 (exploratory)

As preparation for the final part of TU100, I would like you to spend a few minutes thinking about engagement with digital technologies. Do you agree with Champion for Digital Inclusion Martha Lane Fox when she says 'I don't think you can be a proper citizen of our society in the future if you are not engaged online'? If that is the case then should people be forced to go online for their own benefit? Should information technology education be compulsory in the same way that learning to read and write is considered necessary? Or should we continue to think of it as a matter of choice?

Write a few notes expressing your own opinion on the matter and add them to your learning journal. Keep them in mind when you read the next part.

6.5 Conclusion

In this session, I've tried to confront some of the difficult questions that I began with. Despite the complexities involved, I've attempted a few tentative answers, which in turn seem only to raise more questions.

- **Can the digital divide be bridged?**

  Maybe, but there are many obstacles. The spread of technology is not solely dependent on income. As you learned from the Nepal videos, issues as diverse as a reliable supply of power and making information available in a native language place restrictions on the rate at which technology is adopted.

- **Is bridging the digital divide desirable?**

  Issues such as the above can be resolved, given great time and effort, but beyond these lie profound social issues – sometimes built on thousands of years of culture – that restrict people's freedom and desire to use ICTs. Giving people access to technology might mean forcibly transforming society, something that is not generally considered acceptable in democratic cultures. Even when there are no cultural restrictions on people's use of technology, its presence might disrupt society in unforeseen manners.

- **Can technology cure poverty?**

  Undoubtedly technology can bring benefits to individuals, and you have seen examples in this part. However, poverty is generally the result of many interacting factors, not all of which are amenable to technological solutions. At best, the question is naïve; perhaps we should hope that technology will alleviate some aspects of poverty.

- **Does it really matter?**

  Well, that is a question for all of us, not just developing nations. *My digital life* is *your* life; it's *our* lives. What does, will and should the digital society mean to us, now and in the future? Where is technology taking us? You will turn to these questions in the next and final part of the module.

This session should have helped you with the following learning outcomes.

- Describe the concept of a digital divide and some of its different aspects.
- Describe some of the social, political and economic factors influencing the digital divide.
- Use appropriate statistical techniques to analyse aspects of various digital divides.
- Locate, evaluate and use information on the Web.

Summary

In this part you have discovered that the superficially simple concept of a digital divide actually masks a large number of profound issues. In fact there are any number of digital divides, both between countries and between communities and individuals. Rather than a single problem, the digital divide is a multitude of related but different issues.

You were able to explore the presence and depth of the divide using statistical techniques. The most profound divides appear to be based on the state of development of a country; those with highly developed economies appear to have the highest uptake of technology, whilst less well developed economies struggle to provide their citizens with basic services. You saw how non-technological factors – such as lack of access to disposable income, education and energy, and even a diverse culture – can cause problems for the widespread adoption of digital technologies.

You looked at the application and development of technologies inside developing countries, at which point I also introduced the concept of appropriate technology. In many cases, the mobile phone has become the centrepiece of technological innovation in that it is cheap, simple to use and – thanks to near-universal networks – can be used almost anywhere. Projects as diverse as Infoladies and M-PESA are examples of appropriate technology that, whilst partially funded by outside agencies, have been designed to serve the needs of the indigenous population.

At the other extreme, you explored how advanced countries are using digital technologies to create entirely new economies. Estonia is an example of how technology is being used to improve the range of government services, whilst South Korea is creating technologies with the intention of selling goods and services abroad so as to remain a major industrial power.

Digital divides also appear within communities. You saw how the UK government has attempted to identify divides and create a strategy for narrowing or eliminating those divides. The original plan has been modified as the result of the election of a new government and the constriction of government funding, but there is a consistent plan to bridge the country's digital divides.

Finally, I asked some profound questions about the presence of the digital divide and how we go about eliminating it. Once again, it became clear that the divide is not a simple problem; it exists alongside many others including poverty, lack of access to resources and education, political and cultural power, and the roles of government and private industry. Attempts have been made to bridge the divide, but their success has been limited and open to criticism.

The digital divide affects every one of us to a certain extent. We might be members of a group struggling with modern technology, or we may be lucky enough to be fully conversant with technology and have the resources to use it. But billions of people are not lucky enough even to have the choice whether to go online, send an email, make a phone call or browse the Web. Surely it is worth persevering until everyone has the opportunity to engage – or not?

Activity 39 (exploratory)

You are now nearing the end of your study of TU100, so this is the point at which I would like you to return for a final time to the 'How digital is your life?' quiz that you completed in Blocks 1 and 3. Remember, there are no right or wrong answers to this quiz, but taking it once more should help you to gauge how various aspects of your digital life have changed over the course of the module.

If you can access the TU100 website at this moment, please go to the 'Study resources' section and work through the quiz for the third time. It doesn't matter if you can't attempt it straight away, but please try to do it soon.

Comment

Having completed the quiz three times, you will be given some feedback on how your digital life has changed over the course of studying TU100. Whether your life has become more or less digital, or stayed the same, I hope you feel that you have developed new skills to help you survive in the digital world of the future.

Answers to self-assessment activities

Activity 2

The most obvious aspect illustrated by the graph is the huge disparity between those countries with the highest level of access and those with the lowest.

Activity 3

Although there is no clear division between colours, you can clearly see that the left-hand side of the chart – representing countries with the highest levels of access – is dominated by the blue shading for Europe, whilst the right-hand side with the lowest levels is predominantly red – the colour for Africa. We know that European countries are predominantly wealthy and African countries generally poor, so the chart suggests that the number of people in a country connected to the internet is somehow related to how wealthy that country is.

Activity 6

Yes. You should remember from Block 2 Part 5 that correlation does not necessarily imply causation. The correlation between HDI and internet access may arise from all sorts of hidden causal factors – or it might be complete coincidence.

Activity 10

Amongst other factors, you might have identified the following.
- The mesh uses available resources to meet a demand for communication amongst very poor people.
- Being centred on existing facilities, it is local to the people who need to use it.

Activity 11

Because the system is based on mesh telephony, the more nodes there are, the more alternative routes a call can take if a node fails.

Activity 14

The first and most obvious point is that Estonia began with a lower level of adoption than the more developed economies of Finland, Sweden and the UK, but quickly rose to match them and at one point outstripped all three. The steepness of the line shows the rate of change – the steeper the gradient, the faster mobile phones are being adopted. One plausible explanation for this is that the fall of Communism created a huge market of consumers without access to mobile technology and with unsatisfactory fixed-line communications.

Secondly, the rate of take-up of mobile phones has generally been faster in the ex-Soviet republics (Estonia, Latvia, Lithuania and the Russian Federation) than in the UK, Sweden and Finland. Again, this could be explained by the fact that fixed lines in the prosperous non-Communist states were already efficient and plentiful, so there was less temptation for individuals to move to mobile communications.

Activity 16

Amongst other factors, you should have identified the following.

- Village Phone meets the needs of very poor people for communication.
- A phone can be made reasonably local to a user, thus not requiring the user to travel to get access.
- The system is accessible: a user does not need to be rich enough to afford a phone of their own.
- The system is not intrusive: a phone can be used even by people with no permanent home of their own.

Activity 23

I thought of the following.

1. It addresses an existing need (banking).
2. It suits relatively low-value transactions (withdrawals from shops, for example).
3. It uses a relatively low-cost technology that has already been widely adopted.
4. The agent infrastructure is built on an existing network of shops, etc.
5. The agents are already trusted inside the community.

Activity 24

The Netherlands has much more internet capacity and faster connections than most of Africa. This means that the site can serve a high number of simultaneous visitors who will be demanding large amounts of information such as streaming music.

Activity 30

No, the computer will have authenticated Mikk's e-votes using the digital certificate on his ID card. It will recognise that both votes come from the same voter and delete his first vote (for Hele), replacing it with his second vote (for Eliisabet).

Activity 32

(a) Firstly, rising water levels upstream might not affect a community as much as the same floodwaters further down the river, so the inhabitants may not feel obliged to send a warning to downstream communities. Secondly, people do not – or may not want to – go out in the heavy rain that causes flooding.

(b) The following components are vital to the system:

   (i)   water level sensors

   (ii)   modems

   (iii) radio networks using the free 144 MHz wavelength

   (iv) one or more offices containing networked laptops.

(c) Communications costs (such as those for mobile phones) would make the system reliant on continued funding, which may be uncertain.

(d) Problems included the lack of local supplies of PVC piping needed to protect parts of the system, theft of wiring for its scrap value and vandalism.

(e) The community has expert knowledge of the flood patterns of individual rivers that could not be found in academic sources or simply by visiting the site. The government must be involved to coordinate evacuation and relief efforts in the event of a flood.

(f) Yes, this system has all the attributes of a ubiquitous computing system as described in Block 2 Part 2. As you should remember, Weiser's original definition of a ubiquitous computer required such a system to include three distinct technologies:

   (i)   cheap, low-power computers (water level sensors might be computers in their own right, but even if they are nothing more than simple water level gauges, computation is performed by the laptop computers)

   (ii)   a network (radio)

   (iii) software running ubiquitous applications (monitoring and displaying up-to-date sensor values).

Glossary

ad hoc network   A type of network that does not rely on fixed connections. Ad hoc networks do not have any centralised routers; instead, each node can act as its own router. Nodes in an ad hoc network can join or leave the network at any time, with the remaining nodes finding new routes for traffic – the network is said to be self-healing. An example of an ad hoc network is a mesh network.

appropriate technology   A technological solution that takes account of the actual cultural, political and economic circumstances of people, aiming to improve their wellbeing whilst putting as little strain as possible on their environment or finances, and causing minimal disruption to their everyday lives.

cantenna   A **waveguide** made from a discarded metal food can containing a normal Wi-Fi antenna.

community network   A computer network used to provide connectivity across an entire community. In many cases this can be implemented using **mesh networking**.

digital certificate   A public key that has been digitally signed as belonging to the person who claims to own it.

digital divide   (1) The gulf between people who have access to, and the resources to use, ICTs and those who do not. (2) The gulf between people who have the skills, knowledge and abilities to use ICTs and those who do not.

fibre-to-the-building (FTTB)   A network in which the optical fibre runs only as far as the boundary of a multi-tenanted building, with links to individual apartments or offices using alternative technologies. Also known as *fibre-to-the-basement*.

fibre-to-the-cabinet (FTTC)   A network in which the optical fibre runs only as far as a street-side cabinet or under-pavement switch, with individual homes and offices being connected using copper wires no more than 300 m long. Also known as *fibre-to-the-curb*.

fibre-to-the-home (FTTH)   A network in which the optical fibre runs all the way to an individual home. The internal network will use technologies such as Ethernet or wireless connections.

fibre-to-the-node (FTTN)   A network in which the optical fibre runs only as far as a street-side cabinet or small exchange, with the remainder of the network being connected using copper cables more than 300 m long.

fibre-to-the-premises (FTTP) A network in which the optical fibre runs all the way to an individual premises such as an office. The internal network will use technologies such as Ethernet or wireless connections.

Final Third The 17 million UK citizens – generally the poor, elderly and ethnic minorities – without access to a computer.

gateway A device that converts from one protocol to another in order to send data between different types of network.

GDP per capita The **GDP** of a country divided by the number of citizens in that country. Also known as *GDP per head*.

global digital divide Gross inequalities of ICT access and skills between nations.

gross domestic product (GDP) The total value of the goods and services produced by a country in one year.

Human Development Index (HDI) A measure (between 0 and 1) of the prosperity of a country based on a number of indicators such as life expectancy, literacy levels, educational attainment and standard of living.

indicator A measure of some quantity relating to human wellbeing, such as life expectancy, access to health care or education provision.

mesh network An example of an **ad hoc network** usually implemented using wireless technologies. Mesh networks can be used to share scarce resources such as printers or links to the internet amongst a large number of computers.

mesh telephony A situation in which a mesh network, rather than a wired or cellular network, is used to carry telephone calls.

microcredit Small sums of money lent without security to individuals or groups in order to establish businesses or for basic necessities.

mobile banking Banking in which services are provided through a mobile phone. Also known as *M-banking*.

node An individual computer or device in a network. A node may be a general-purpose computer, a router or a switch.

not spot A rural area with little or no access to high-speed internet.

PC bangs South Korean cyber cafés offering high-speed internet access.

scatter chart A visual representation of how well two sets of values are correlated with one another.

self-healing A term used to characterise mesh networks, referring to the fact that when one computer leaves the network or crashes, others will continue to direct traffic.

supernode   A special type of node found in some mesh networks. Supernodes are often responsible for connecting to outside networks. The supernode software is usually run on a more powerful computer than other nodes in the network.

waveguide   A device that directs wireless signals in a precise direction.

References

Borland, J. (2007) 'Online Voting Clicks in Estonia', *Wired* [online], 2 March, http://www.wired.com/politics/security/news/2007/03/72846 (accessed 6 June 2011).

Bowlby, C. (2009) 'The internet's conscientious objectors', *BBC News* [online], 6 August, http://news.bbc.co.uk/1/hi/magazine/8187305.stm (accessed 6 June 2011).

Evans, J. (2009) 'One Laptop Per Child: What Went Wrong', entry on *The Walrus Blog* [online], 19 January, http://www.walrusmagazine.com/blogs/2009/01/19/one-laptop-per-child-what-went-wrong/ (accessed 6 June 2011).

FAIR (2007) *Scathing criticism from FAIR for "One Laptop Per Child"* [online], press release, January, http://www.fairinternational.org/fi-artikkel_229.nml (accessed 6 June 2011).

Gillwald, A. and Stork, C. (2008) *Towards Evidence-based ICT Policy and Regulation: ICT access and usage in Africa*, Volume One 2008 Policy Paper Two, ResearchICTAfrica; also available online at http://www.researchictafrica.net/publications.php (accessed 6 June 2011).

Grameen Foundation (n.d.) *Empowering the Poor* [online], http://www.grameenfoundation.org/what-we-do/technology/empowering-poor (accessed 6 June 2011).

Hargittai, E. (2003) 'The digital divide and what to do about it' in Jones, D.C. (ed.) *The New Economy Handbook*, San Diego, CA, Academic Press.

HM Government (2008) *Delivering Digital Inclusion: An Action Plan for Consultation*, London, Crown Copyright; also available online at http://www.communities.gov.uk/publications/communities/deliveringdigitalinclusion (accessed 6 June 2011).

International Monetary Fund (2011) *World Economic Outlook Database* [online], http://www.imf.org/external/pubs/ft/weo/2011/01/weodata/index.aspx (accessed 6 June 2011).

Kumar, D. (2009) 'Two-wheel triumph', The Guardian [online], 23 November, http://www.guardian.co.uk/journalismcompetition/professional-two-wheel-triumph (accessed 6 June 2011).

Lamb, P.J. (2007) 'Technology and the New Imperialism', *OhmyNews* [online], 11 December, http://english.ohmynews.com/articleview/article_view.asp?menu=c10400&no=381209&rel_no=1 (accessed 6 June 2011).

Mehra, B., Merkel, C. and Bishop, A.P. (2004) 'The internet for empowerment of minority and marginalized users', *New Media & Society*, vol. 6, no. 6, pp. 781–802.

Moss, J. (2002) 'Power and the digital divide', *Ethics and Information Technology*, vol. 4, no. 2, pp. 159–65.

Musil, S. (2009) 'OLPC slashes workforce in half, cuts salaries', *CNet News* [online], 7 January, http://news.cnet.com/8301-1001_3-10135779-92.html (accessed 6 June 2011).

NTIA (1999) *Falling Through the Net: Defining the Digital Divide*, National Telecommunications & Information Administration, US Department of Commerce; also available online at http://www.ntia.doc.gov/ntiahome/fttn99/contents.html (accessed 6 June 2011).

Smith, S. (2005) 'The $100 laptop – is it a wind-up?', *CCN International* [online], 1 December, http://edition.cnn.com/2005/WORLD/africa/12/01/laptop/ (accessed 6 June 2011).

United Nations Development Programme (n.d.) 'HDI value', *International Human Development Indicators* [online], http://hdrstats.undp.org/en/indicators/49806.html (accessed 6 June 2011).

Wikipedia (2011) 'Digital divide' in *Wikipedia: the free encyclopedia* [online], http://en.wikipedia.org/wiki/Digital_divide (accessed 24 April 2011).

World Economic Forum (2002) *Annual Report of the Global Digital Divide Initiative*, Geneva, World Economic Forum.

Acknowledgements

Grateful acknowledgement is made to the following sources.

Text
Quotations pp. 44 and 45: Kumar, D. (2009) 'Two-wheel triumph', Guardian News & Media Limited

Figures
Figure 3: © www.thenextweb.com

Figure 4: Taken from www.flickr.com/Steve Song and used under http://creativecommons.org/licenses/by-nc-sa/2.0/

Figure 5: Taken from http://wirelessafrica.meraka.org.za

Figure 6: Taken from http://wirelessafrica.org

Figure 7: Taken from www.atcom.cn

Figure 10: © Grameen Bank

Figure 11: © Grameen Bank

Figure 12: © PILBIIKS & D.Net

Figure 14: © IDG Communications

Figure 15: © www.textually.org

Figure 16(a): © Grundfos Management A/S

Figure 16(b): From www.grundfoslifelink.com

Figure 17: © www.africaunsigned.com

Figure 18: © LG Appliances

Figure 19: © Kia Hendry/Flickr.com/photos/16105436. This file is licensed under the Creative Commons Attribution ShareAlike 2.0, http://creative commons.org/licenses/by/2.0/deed/en

Figure 20: © Taken from en.wikipedia.org/wiki/File:Incheon_Skyline.jpg. This file is licensed under the Creative Commons Attribution ShareAlike 2.0, http//creativecommons.org/licenses/by/2.0/deed.en

Figure 21: © With kind permission of Apis Services

Figure 22: © swedbank.ee

Figure 24: © www.swedbank.ee

Figure 25: © swedbank.ee

Figure 26: © Uhendatud Piletite AS

Figure 27: © www.cellbazaar.com

Figure 28(a): © NASA

Figure 29: Copyright © US National Oceanic and Atmospheric Administration